HCISPP Study Guide

HCISPP Study Guide

Timothy Virtue
Justin Rainey

ELSEVIER

AMSTERDAM • BOSTON • HEIDELBERG • LONDON
NEW YORK • OXFORD • PARIS • SAN DIEGO
SAN FRANCISCO • SINGAPORE • SYDNEY • TOKYO
Syngress Publishers is an imprint of Elsevier

Acquiring Editor: Chris Katsaropoulos
Editorial Project Manager: Benjamin Rearick
Project Manager: Surya Narayanan Jayachandran
Designer: Maria Ines Cruz

Syngress is an imprint of Elsevier
225 Wyman Street, Waltham, MA 02451, USA

British Library Cataloguing-in-Publication Data
A catalogue record for this book is available from the British Library

Library of Congress Cataloging-in-Publication Data
A catalog record for this book is available from the Library of Congress

ISBN: 978-0-12-802043-2

For information on all Syngress publications
visit our website at http://store.elsevier.com/

Working together
to grow libraries in
developing countries

www.elsevier.com • www.bookaid.org

Dedication

To my wife Jill – Your unconditional support and love make me the luckiest man alive. Thanks for sharing your life with me.

To my late grandpa Justin O'Connell whose 45 years of dedication teaching English at the University of Minnesota served as my inspiration to write this book.

Justin

To my late grandmothers Claire and Stella who showed me the importance of living life to the fullest, and that with passion and true grit, anything is possible.

Tim

Contents

Author Bio

Justin C. Rainey (CISSP, CIPP/US) is a global information security, privacy and technology risk management leader whose entire professional career has focused on the protection of nonpublic information. Justin began his career in 1998 providing security and technical support for an independent school district, and over the past 16 years, gained security and privacy experience in various areas including healthcare, research, education, telecommunications, retail, banking, insurance, and investment management. He currently serves as information security manager for a global investment management firm and is pursuing a bachelor of science degree in Political Science at the University of Houston. Justin resides in Houston, Texas with his wife Jill and their two dogs Austin and Mariette.

Tim Virtue (HCISPP, CISSP, CIPP/G, CISA, CCSK, CFE, CSM) is a global information security, privacy and risk management executive. Tim has extensive experience with publicly traded global corporations, privately held businesses, government agencies, and nonprofit organizations of all types and sizes. Tim holds an executive master of science in information systems technology degree from George Washington University and a bachelors of science in Criminal Justice degree with a concentration in security management from Northeastern University. He currently serves as the chief information security officer (CISO) for Texas.gov.

Technical Editor Bio

Jason Adamson (CEH, CISSP) is information security director for Voya Financial Services focusing on penetration testing, application code review, and other kinds of security testing. He has been working to protect PII and company sensitive data for 15 years and has worked for companies in financial, manufacturing, retail, and telecommunications sectors. Jason holds a degree in computer engineering technologies from Southern Polytechnic State University.

Preface

We are living in unprecedented times. This environment of constant change and transformation offers both opportunities and challenges. The opportunities and societal advances offered by healthcare technology are abundant. However, these advancements come with privacy and security concerns. We do not advocate fearing such change simply because of the privacy and security concerns. In fact, we look forward to all of the benefits and embrace the change, as long as society can find a way to balance the risks against the rewards. As we transition some of our most valued personal health information to various healthcare technology systems, there is and always will be a critical need for Information Security and Privacy professionals in the healthcare field.

There is a significant shortage of qualified professionals who truly understand all the aspects of Information Security and Privacy, including what it takes to develop, implement, and maintain an effective program while supporting the business needs of the organization and delivering leading-edge healthcare. We have seen a plethora of new threat actors enter the arena in an attempt to exploit vulnerable systems with various motives. These actors include foreign governments, "hacktivists," organized crime, cyber criminals, and even competitors in an attempt to gain a strategic advantage. The sophistication and scale of attacks surpass anything we've seen over the past decade and protecting healthcare organizations becomes more difficult as new technologies are adopted. This contributes to an insatiable demand for qualified Information Security and Privacy professionals.

Why focus on the Healthcare industry? Healthcare is growing at an unprecedented pace and is increasingly vulnerable as the industry shifts to electronic healthcare records.

The following is a list of key issues we believe will drive information security and privacy activities within the Healthcare industry and contribute to the demand for qualified professionals.

1. The Healthcare industry is extremely fragmented with minimal standards for interoperability and data sharing between hospitals, pharmacy benefit management companies, insurance companies, and

pharmacies. These issues are actively being addressed, but require a significant investment in technology. With increasing connectivity and access to systems and data, risks will also increase. Connectivity in the form of health information exchanges (HITS) and accountable care organizations also drives demand for qualified professionals.

2. There has been huge underinvestment in technology and especially for providers with most investments focused on providing or improving patient care. Old (legacy) systems remain a major security concern as many contain ePHI and need to be secured as they are updated or replaced.

3. There are enormous amounts of healthcare fraud and abuse within the industry, causing costs to spiral out of control. Technology in conjunction with security and privacy controls can provide solutions to increase business visibility and assist with managing these risks.

4. Demand for healthcare is exploding commensurate with the rapidly aging baby boomer population. This will require expansion of existing systems and implementation of new technologies to improve productivity and outcomes.

5. It is projected that the United States will experience a shortage of 160,000 doctors over the next 20 years and the industry will have to find new ways of improving doctor productivity. This will require implementation of new and innovative technologies that need to be secured.

6. Regulators have been aggressive in regulating the security and privacy of Healthcare IT systems and issuing fines for noncompliance.

7. Despite having vast amounts of sensitive data, healthcare Information Security programs are far behind that of Financial Services and other similarly situated industries. The FBI has also issued warnings to the Healthcare industry to urgently improve their programs and controls.

8. The Bureau of Labor Statistics (BLS) projects the job market for Information Security professionals to expand by 37% between 2012 and 2022. Information Security is one of the fastest-growing professions in the job market.

There are a vast number of opportunities for qualified healthcare Information Security and Privacy professionals. The HealthCare Certified Information Security and Privacy Practitioner (HCISPP) credential will certify your knowledge and stature as a qualified professional. There will be vast opportunities for those who prepare for the future, and this book is your first step toward a rewarding healthcare information security and privacy professional.

Acknowledgments

Justin would like to thank his wife, Jill, for her patience and support throughout the writing of this book. Thanks to co-author Tim Virtue and technical editor Jason Adamson for their contributions and collaboration on this work. And finally thanks to his family for their support: Kathleen Rainey, Edward Rainey, Scott Britain, and Dan and Allison Connally.

I would like to thank my family, friends, educators, and industry colleagues. Without your support, guidance, and mentorship over the years, I would not have the inspiration, expertise, or ability to write this book. I would also like to give a special thanks to co-author Justin Rainey, technical editor Jason Adamson, and the team at Elsevier. If not for their hard work, dedication, and support, we would not have had this book today.

CHAPTER 1

Introduction

THIS CHAPTER WILL HELP READERS UNDERSTAND

- Importance of information security and privacy
- Target audience
- HealthCare Information Security and Privacy Practitioner (HCISPP) certification requirements
- Learning objectives

BACKGROUND

The importance of security and privacy is rapidly increasing across all industries, especially given a recent acceleration in public data breach and record disclosures. As this book was composed the public has witnessed large breaches within the retail industry involving stolen credit card and personal information. At first glance one might discard this type of threat as not applicable to healthcare organizations given their core business involves the delivery of patient care. In many cases they might be wrong given patients regularly pay for healthcare services using a credit or debit card, the massive amount of personal health information (PHI) within the organization, a significant increase in the use of health information technology (which creates additional privacy and security risk), and PHI being shared outside organizational boundaries with third parties to support the delivery of healthcare services. Healthcare organizations will need qualified risk management professionals to assist with managing the broad array of risks faced within the industry. The HCISPP certification is for individuals who want to understand how to assess risk and implement and maintain security and privacy controls specific to the healthcare industry while being compliant with the many laws and regulations that govern the healthcare industry. Individuals with certifications such as the HCISPP are more likely to be selected for job interviews based on the immediate recognition of an industry certification and the qualifications it conveys. Since the

1

exam details are subject to change, per (ISC)^2, we encourage candidates to obtain the most current HCISPP Candidate Information Bulletin available from (ISC)2 prior to beginning their exam preparation. Candidates may require a deeper understanding of some concepts discussed throughout this book depending on the nature of their current or future roles, educational background, and work experience in each of the specific HCISPP exam domains. However, this book was written to provide a foundational level of knowledge and teach candidates only what is necessary to pass the HCISPP examination – nothing more, nothing less. Consider this the first step in a journey, as a security and privacy practitioner in the healthcare industry. Since the healthcare industry, the technology that supports it, and the laws and regulations that govern it continuously change we encourage HCISPP candidates and certificate holders to actively participate in the industry, stay abreast of changes, and commit to continuing education and gaining new experiences. The examination and this book focus on six key domains of knowledge:

- Healthcare industry
- Regulatory environment
- Privacy and security in healthcare
- Information governance and risk management
- Information risk assessment
- Third-party risk management

Individuals who may want to consider obtaining a HCISPP certification include, but are not limited to:

- Information security analysts
- Information security officers (CSO, CISO, ISO)
- Privacy officers (CPO)
- Compliance officers (CCO)
- Records management personnel
- Information technology managers
- Security and privacy consultants
- Risk management personnel
- Internal and external auditors
- Data protection officers
- Health information managers

HCISPP Certification Requirements

Prior to taking the HCISPP examination, candidates must meet the following requirements:

- Register for the exam and pay the examination fee. The most current fees are available at https://www.isc2.org/certification-register-now.aspx.

- Have a minimum of 2 years' security, privacy, and compliance experience in one of the six knowledge domains. At least 1 year of experience is required in one of the following three domains:
  - Healthcare industry
  - Regulatory environment in healthcare
  - Privacy and security in healthcare

The second year of experience can be in the domains mentioned earlier or in one of the following three domains:

- Information governance and risk management
- Information risk assessment
- Third-party risk management

Legal and information management experience may also be substituted for compliance and privacy experience, respectively.

- Provide a truthful attestation of professional experience and legally agree to abide by the Code of Ethics; and
- Provide yes or no responses to four questions pertaining to criminal history and background.

Exam Registration

The exam is computer-based (CBT) and proctored at an authorized location, while paper-based exams are available on a case-by-case basis. The exam will consist of 125 multiple choice questions with 4 potential choices and must be completed in 3 h. Candidates should ensure sufficient rest prior to the examination, and if traveling from outside the area, consider staying at a hotel close to the testing facility the night beforehand. Registration for the exam can be completed online through the (ISC)2 website or over the phone and requires payment of the exam fee, agreement to the Code of Ethics, and responses to criminal history and background questions.

Code of Ethics

The Code of Ethics includes a preamble and four cannons focused on ethics. All professionals who receive an HCISPP certification must abide by the Code, recognize their certification is a privilege (not a right), and understand the certification is subject to revocation for members who intentionally or knowingly violate the Code.

Preamble

The safety and welfare of society and the common good, duty to our principals, and to each other, requires that we adhere, and be seen to adhere, to the highest ethical standards of behavior. Therefore, strict adherence to this Code is a condition of certification.

Code of Ethics Cannons

- Protect society, the common good, necessary public trust and confidence, and the infrastructure.
- Act honorably, honestly, justly, responsibly, and legally.
- Provide diligent and competent service to principals.
- Advance and protect the profession.

Healthcare Industry

HEALTHCARE SYSTEMS

Healthcare is delivered in a number and variety of ways in today's modern healthcare system. Healthcare services range from being delivered by an individual physician to a global pharmaceutical company. In addition to a wide range and structure of healthcare providers, there are also a large number of third parties (vendors, business partners, etc.) that provide a range of support services (e.g., medical equipment suppliers, billing, technology). Another critical component of the healthcare system is the various government agencies and regulators.

HEALTHCARE ORGANIZATIONS

Organizations providing healthcare can be structured in a variety of ways, but are commonly classified into either for-profit or not-for-profit organizations. Each type of entity has its own objectives and challenges, but the underlying commonality is the delivery of high-quality healthcare services at a low cost. Healthcare costs have significantly increased in recent years and the costs are anticipated to continuously rise over the next several years. Healthcare organizations may also be impacted by their physical and jurisdictional locations, the specific types of healthcare services they deliver, and country-specific legal and regulatory requirements.

5

HEALTHCARE PROVIDER

The U.S. Department of Health and Human Services (HHS) recognizes definitions for both healthcare providers and covered entities:

- **Healthcare provider** – A provider of medical or health services and any other person or organization who furnishes, bills, or is paid for healthcare in the normal course of business.
- **Health Insurance Portability and Accountability Act of 1996 (HIPAA)– covered entity** – Any organization or corporation that directly handles personal health information (PHI) or personal health records (PHRs).

ORGANIZED PHYSICIAN SERVICES

Organized physician services evolved from single practitioner service model to provide more comprehensive care by an organization. This model enables an independent organization to deliver scalable patient care services that are not possible by a single physician.

THE NATIONAL PROVIDER IDENTIFIER (NPI)

The NPI is a unique 10-character identification number for covered healthcare providers. Its purpose is to improve the efficiency and effectiveness of the electronic transmission of health information and is mandated as part of the Administrative Simplification provisions of the HIPAA. The Centers for Medicare & Medicaid Services (CMS) has developed the National Plan and Provider Enumeration System (NPPES), which is responsible for the assignment and administration of these unique identifiers.

PHARMACEUTICAL INDUSTRY

The pharmaceutical industry is composed of various types of enterprises that produce medicine and drugs used in the delivery of healthcare. It is important to note that in most cases, pharmaceutical companies do not deliver medicine and drugs directly to patients. Furthermore, pharmaceutical companies are heavily regulated and must adhere to a variety of laws and regulations regarding the research, testing, marketing, and production of drugs to ensure proper use and patient safety. Closely related are the organizations (commonly referred to as pharmacies) responsible for the direct medicine and drug distribution.

PAYERS

A payer in healthcare generally refers to entities other than the patient that finance or reimburse the cost of healthcare services. There are a number and variety of types of organizations that meet these criteria, but some of the more common types of entities include insurance companies, healthcare service contractors, self-insured organizations providing healthcare, and governments making payments for healthcare services.

A healthcare provider sends claims to a health plan to request payment for medical services.

ELECTRONIC DATA INTERCHANGE (EDI)

According to the HHS, EDI "Is the electronic transfer of information, such as electronic media health claims, in a standard format between trading partners. EDI allows entities within the health care system to exchange medical, billing, and other information and to process transactions in a manner, which is fast and cost effective. With EDI there is a substantial reduction in handling and processing time compared to paper, and the risk of lost paper documents is eliminated. EDI can eliminate the inefficiencies of handling paper documents, which will significantly reduce administrative burden; lower operating costs, and improves overall data quality." Under HIPAA, the following standard transactions must use EDI:

- Claims and encounter information
- Payment and remittance advice
- Claims status
- Eligibility
- Enrollment and disenrollment
- Referrals and authorizations
- Coordination of benefits
- Premium payment

Additionally, under HIPAA, the following specific code sets for diagnoses and procedures must also be used:

- Healthcare Common Procedure Coding System (HCPCS) (Ancillary Services/Procedures)
- CPT-4 (Physicians' Procedures)
- CDT (Dental Terminology)
- ICD-9 (Diagnosis and Hospital Inpatient Procedures)
- ICD-10 (As of October 1, 2014)
- National Drug Codes (NDC)

VALUE-ADDED NETWORKS (VANs)

Many healthcare organizations choose to work with VANs to aid in EDI. A VAN is a hosted service offering that acts as an intermediary between business partners such as hospitals and insurance payers. It simplifies the communications process by reducing the number of parties with which a company needs to facilitate EDI. VANs can offer a variety of support services for EDI and related activities and healthcare organizations should select the services most appropriate to their specific operating and regulatory models.

HEALTH INSURANCE EXCHANGES

Health insurance exchanges are centralized health insurance offerings available to individuals who do not currently have healthcare insurance. The exchanges are typically subsidized and/or managed by government program, the largest example being HealthCare.gov. These exchanges typically offer competitive rates since insurers are spreading risk among a larger population and can offer "group" discounts and rates. Health insurance exchanges are supported by the U.S. government, and are the foundation of the Affordable Care Act.

BUSINESS ASSOCIATES

Since most healthcare service providers focus on delivering patient care, they look to other organizations to provide the necessary business support activities associated with modern healthcare delivery. Some common examples of business associates include accounting and financial services, claims processors, transcription services, consultants, etc. Under the HIPAA Privacy Rule, covered providers and health plans are allowed to disclose protected health information to business associates if the providers or plans obtain satisfactory assurances that the business associate will comply with the following practices to ensure patient information is properly safeguarded:

- Use the information only for the purposes for which it was engaged by the covered entity.
- Safeguard the information from misuse.
- Help the covered entity comply with some of the covered entity's duties under the HIPAA Privacy Rule.

HEALTH INFORMATION TECHNOLOGY (HIT)

According to the HHS, HIT "Involves the exchange of health information in an electronic environment. Widespread use of health IT within the health care industry will improve the quality of health care, prevent medical errors, reduce health care costs, increase administrative efficiencies, decrease paperwork, and expand access to affordable health care." Some of the more common components include electronic medical records (EMRs), clinical decision support systems (CDSS), and computerized physician order entry (CPOE). In addition to HIT being used directly for the delivery of patient care services, healthcare organizations also use HIT for management and business support functions.

MEDICAL DEVICES

Medical devices are an integral part for many organizations' delivery of today's modern healthcare treatments and services. The World Health Organization (WHO) defines a medical device as "An article, instrument, apparatus or machine that is used in the prevention, diagnosis or treatment of illness or disease, or for detecting, measuring, restoring, correcting or modifying the structure or function of the body for some health purpose." Types of medical devices often include self-care, electronic, diagnostic, surgical, durable medical equipment, acute care, emergency and trauma, long-term care, storage, and transport. Due to the varied types and widespread use of medical devices, healthcare organizations have a responsibility to properly protect patients and their associated health data when using medical devices for patient care. The U.S. Food and Drug Administration formally acknowledges and classifies medical devices. According to the FDA website, "The Food and Drug Administration (FDA) has established classifications for approximately 1,700 different generic types of devices and grouped them into 16 medical specialties referred to as panels. Each of these generic types of devices is assigned to one of three regulatory classes based on the level of control necessary to assure the safety and effectiveness of the device. The three classes and the requirements, which apply, to them are:

Device Class and Regulatory Controls

1. Class I General Controls
   a. With Exemptions
   b. Without Exemptions
2. Class II General Controls and Special Controls
   a. With Exemptions
   b. Without Exemptions
3. Class III General Controls and Premarket Approval."

MEANINGFUL USE REGULATIONS

One of the most important changes to the U.S. healthcare system, and a significant driver of HIT, is meaningful use (MU). According to HealthIT.gov, "The Medicare and Medicaid Electronic Health Record (EHR) Incentive Programs provide financial incentives for the 'meaningful use' of certified EHR technology. To receive an EHR incentive payment, providers have to show that they are 'meaningfully using' their certified EHR technology by meeting certain measurement thresholds that range from recording patient information as structured data to exchanging summary care records."

There are a variety of organizational benefits to the adoption of electronic health record (EHR) technology and MU. Some of the more common benefits include accurate and updated information, and increased accessibility to both patients and healthcare providers.

ELECTRONIC HEALTH RECORD

EHRs are the new cornerstone of today's modern healthcare delivery and management. According to the Healthcare Information and Management Systems Society (HIMSS), "The Electronic Health Record (EHR) is a longitudinal electronic record of patient health information generated by one or more encounters in any care delivery setting. Included in this information are patient demographics, progress notes, problems, medications, vital signs, past medical history, immunizations, laboratory data and radiology reports. The EHR automates and streamlines the clinician's workflow. The EHR has the ability to generate a complete record of a clinical patient encounter – as well as supporting other care-related activities directly or indirectly via interface – including evidence-based decision support, quality management, and outcomes reporting." As you can see from this very comprehensive definition, the EHR plays a critical role in the overall operations of a healthcare organization and touches upon and often includes a tremendous amount of sensitive information. Therefore, healthcare organizations must understand the elements and information flows of EHRs and implement the appropriate privacy and security safeguards.

PERSONAL HEALTH RECORD

A PHR is very similar to an EHR. The primary difference is that the information and management of the record is managed at the individual patient level. HealthIT.gov states, "A personal health record (PHR) is an electronic application used by patients to maintain and manage their health information in a private, secure, and confidential environment." PHRs:

- Are managed by patients
- Can include information from a variety of sources, including healthcare providers and patients themselves
- Can help patients securely and confidentially store and monitor health information, such as diet plans or data from home monitoring systems, as well as patient contact information, diagnosis lists, medication lists, allergy lists, immunization histories, and much more
- Are separate from, and do not replace, the legal record of any healthcare provider
- Are distinct from portals that simply allow patients to view provider information or communicate with providers

Often times PHRs are associated with EHRs and the information from each type of record can be exchanged across the two record types. For this reason, it is important that the information contained within and the PHRs themselves be properly safeguarded. Healthcare organizations managing the technology supporting PHRs also have the responsibility to protect patient information. Additionally healthcare organizations need to partner with patients to ensure the patient understands their individual roles and responsibilities in managing their healthcare information and a PHR.

HEALTH INSURANCE

In order to comprehensively understand modern healthcare delivery, it is important to discuss the subject of health insurance. There are numerous types of health insurance and patients often have a variety of arrangements they can select from to assist in the payment or reimbursement for healthcare. However, a common theme among most health insurance plans is that an insurer will pay for some or all of the healthcare costs for a patient in exchange for a premium. In fact, HealthCare.gov defines health insurance as "A contract that requires your health insurer to pay some or all of your healthcare costs in exchange for a premium." As indicated earlier, the number of types and specific details of health insurance can vary greatly from organization to organization. The following discussions will highlight some of the more common health insurance programs. However, it is important to note that the details of plans change frequently and organizations outside of the United States often have additional variances in their programs that are specific to the healthcare delivery customs for that country.

Private Health Insurance
Private health insurance is a type of insurance coverage where individuals are responsible for providing their own health insurance coverage. However, in most cases the patient's employer provides all or some of the funding as an employee benefit. Private health insurance is currently the most prevalent form of health insurance in the United States. However, it is important to note that Medicare and Medicaid (two types of public health coverage) are also common in the United States.

Although private health insurance often has a wider network of healthcare providers and services, it often costs considerably more than public health insurance.

Public Health Insurance
The other major type of health insurance is public health insurance. This is an insurance program provided by the government. The primary benefit of a public health insurance program is that it can provide health insurance access and affordability to patients who could not obtain private health

insurance. A major disadvantage of public health insurance is the eligibility requirements often associated with a government-managed health insurance program.

Health Insurance Programs

As discussed earlier, there are a variety of health insurance programs. The specifics arrangements of each program are left to the discretion of the insurer and the patient. A list and high-level description of common health insurance programs in the United States is shown as follows:

Name of Health Insurance Program	Description of Health Insurance Program
Indemnity plan	Patient selects healthcare provider of their choice. The service provider submits a claim to the patient's insurance for services rendered
Health Maintenance Organization (HMOs)	Patient pays a set premium and is entitled services included in the benefit offering. Patients must see a primary care physician within the HMO, and are required to obtain a referral for specialists and additional healthcare services not included in the HMO's primary offering
Preferred provider organizations (PPOs)	A PPO can be considered a hybrid of an indemnity plan and an HMO. Patients can select a healthcare provider of their choice, as long as it is within PPO network. Some PPOs will allow patients to select service outside of the network, but will usually only reimburse patients for a smaller percentage than if they had stayed within the network
Exclusive provider organizations (EPOs)	EPOs are similar to PPOs except that patients will only be reimbursed for healthcare services provided within the network
Point-of-service plans (POS)	A POS is a hybrid between an HMO and a PPO
High-deductible health plan (HDHP)	HDHPs are plans with high deductibles, but these are balanced with very low premiums
Catastrophic health insurance plan	These plans also have high deductibles, but only provide coverage for serious injury or illness
Medicare and Medicaid	U.S. government insurance programs. Medicare provides insurance for the elderly and Medicaid provides insurance for the poor

PAYMENT MODELS

There are a variety of payment models currently available in the healthcare industry. We will provide a high-level perspective as payment for healthcare services is an important component of the overall healthcare system. However, specific program details and operating models vary among organizations and we will focus on some of the more common payment models, which are listed as follows:

- **Fee for service** – Reimbursement for specific, individual services provided to a patient.
- **Pay for coordination** – Payment for specified care coordination services, usually to certain types of providers (e.g., nursing home).
- **Pay for performance** – Defined as a payment or financial incentive (e.g., a bonus) associated with achieving defined and measurable goals related to care processes and outcomes, patient experience, resource use, and other factors.
- **Episode or bundled payments** – Single payments for a group of services related to a treatment or condition that may involve multiple providers in multiple settings.
- **Comprehensive care/total cost of care payment** – A single risk-adjusted payment for the full range of healthcare services needed by a specified group of people for a fixed period of time.

HEALTHCARE CODING

Healthcare coding is essential to the transactional aspect of healthcare delivery. According to the CMS, "Under HIPAA, the Secretary of Health and Human Services (HHS) adopted certain standard transactions for Electronic Data Interchange (EDI) of health care data. These transactions are: claims and encounter information, payment and remittance advice, claims status, eligibility, enrollment and disenrollment, referrals and authorizations, coordination of benefits and premium payment. If a covered entity conducts one of the adopted transactions electronically, they must use the adopted standard – either from ASC X12N or NCPDP (for certain pharmacy transactions). Covered entities must adhere to the content and format requirements of each transaction. Also, under HIPAA, HHS has adopted specific code sets for diagnoses and procedures to be used in all transactions. The HCPCS (Ancillary Services/Procedures), CPT-4 (Physicians Procedures), CDT (Dental Terminology), ICD-9 (Diagnosis and hospital inpatient Procedures), ICD-10 (As of October 1, 2014) and NDC (National Drug Codes) codes with which providers and health plan are familiar, are the adopted code sets for procedures, diagnoses, and drugs."

Medical Coding Systems

Currently there are two medical coding systems used in the United States and include:

- HCPCS:
  - Level I Current Procedural Terminology (CPT) codes and Level II National Codes
- International Classification of Disease (ICD)

The HCPCS is used to report hospital outpatient procedures and physician services.

These coding systems support the healthcare system by providing functions for physician reimbursement, hospital payments, quality review, and the collection of statistical data.

The American Medical Association (AMA) publishes CPT codes. CPT codes are used to report medical procedures and services under public and private health insurance programs. The WHO maintains the ICD classification. Its primary purpose is to categorize diseases for morbidity and mortality reporting. As of this writing the WHO states, "ICD-10 was endorsed by the Forty-third World Health Assembly in May 1990 and came into use in WHO Member States as from 1994. The 11th revision of the classification has already started and will continue until 2017." U.S.-based healthcare organizations should note that the United States has used a clinical modification of ICD (ICD-10-CM) for the additional purposes of reimbursement.

SYSTEMATIZED NOMENCLATURE OF MEDICINE (SNOMED) – CLINICAL TERMS (CT)

According to the International Health Terminology Standards Development Organization (IHTSDO) (the not-for-profit organization that owns, maintains, and distributes SNOMED CT), "SNOMED CT provides the core general terminology for the electronic health record (EHR) and contains more than 311,000 active concepts with unique meanings and formal logic-based definitions organized into hierarchies. When implemented in software applications, SNOMED CT can be used to represent clinically relevant information consistently, reliably and comprehensively as an integral part of producing electronic health records." Healthcare organizations use coding systems to enable aggregation of accounting and medical record data by disease, patient characteristics, or site of care. These systems often include the various patient classification systems such as Diagnosis-Related Groups (DRGs), Ambulatory Patient Groups (APGs), and Resource Utilization Groups (RUGs). The common classification systems are defined as follows:

- **DRG** – Payment approach that focuses on inpatient hospitalizations, setting a price based on categories of illness.
- **APGs** – Encompass a full range of ambulatory settings and designed to explain the amount and type of resources used in an ambulatory visit.
- **Ambulatory Payment Classifications (APCs)** – Used by the U.S. government for hospital services provided to Medicare and Medicaid patients.
- **RUGs** – Relies on specific documentation of patient care delivered, meaning patient resources used.

MEDICAL BILLING

Medical billing is the part of the healthcare process where claims and payment information is managed and communicated with health insurance companies in order for the healthcare provider to receive payment (reimbursement) for services delivered to a patient. After a healthcare provider sees a patient, the diagnosis and procedure codes are assigned accordingly. These codes assist the insurance company in determining coverage and reimbursement for the rendered services.

HIPAA TRANSACTION AND CODE SETS

Under HIPAA, the TCS Standard/Rule mandates uniform electronic interchange formats for all covered entities. The TCS Rule only covers PHI in electronic form and is used with EDI standards and requires their use by all covered entities. It has selected its EDI standards from among the preexisting transaction and code set specifications of a variety of nongovernmental Designated Standards Maintenance Organizations (DSMOs).

The TCS Rule uses the American National Standards Institute (ANSI) Accredited Standards Committee (ASC) X12 transactions (ANSI X12N) standards as follows:

- Health Care Claims or Equivalent Encounter Information (X12N 837)
- Eligibility for a Health Plan (X12N 270/271)
- Referral Certification and Authorization (X12N 278 or NCPDP for retail pharmacy)
- Health Care Claim Status (X12N 276/277)
- Enrollment and Disenrollment in a Health Plan (X12N 834)
- Health Care Payment and Remittance Advice (X12N 835)
- Health Plan Premium Payments (X12N 820)
- Coordination of Benefits (X12N 837 or NCPDP for retail pharmacy)

NATIONAL UNIFORM BILLING COMMITTEE (NUBC)

The NUBC is a voluntary committee whose work is coordinated through the offices of the American Hospital Association (AHA) and includes participation of all the major national provider and payer organizations. The Committee monitors and manages the utilization of this standard uniform (UB) billing form and data set used throughout the industry for billing transactions.

HEALTHCARE CLEARINGHOUSE

Healthcare clearinghouses are organizations that process nonstandard data elements of health information into standard data elements. The clearinghouse receives unstructured healthcare transactions from a healthcare organization and translates the data into the format required and forwards the processed information to the appropriate partner organization (commonly a payer).

WORKFLOW MANAGEMENT

Due to the significant emphasis on healthcare reform and in order to comply with various legal, regulatory, and industry best practices, healthcare organizations work on ways to improve their processes, deliver high-quality care more efficiently, and simultaneously reduce costs. Since many healthcare processes are complex and data intensive, and include both clinical and administrative activities, healthcare organizations are turning to various kinds of workflow management systems to manage healthcare activities. Healthcare organizations are seeking automated solutions and applications that simplify the routine delivery of patient healthcare. Although workflow management systems can vary in type, size, and function from organization to organization, there are several common applications within the healthcare industry. The workflow management applications common to the healthcare industry address routine administrative (billing, claims, etc.) and clinical (patient management, charting, etc.) activities.

REGULATORY ENVIRONMENT

Although Chapter 3 will go into great detail about the specific security, privacy, and oversight issues impacting the healthcare industry, it is important to recognize the overall and significant impact the regulatory environment has on the healthcare industry. Since the healthcare industry is heavily regulated, laws and regulations drive many of an organization's daily operations, in order to safeguard patient health information. Understanding the complexity of the regulatory environment is fundamental to understanding how the healthcare industry is required to deliver services. Additionally, understanding of the regulatory environment allows organizations to develop policies and procedures that simultaneously deliver effective patient care, meet business objectives, and comply with legal and regulatory requirements.

PUBLIC HEALTH REPORTING

According to the HHS, "The HIPAA Privacy Rule recognizes the legitimate need for public health authorities and others responsible for ensuring public health and safety to have access to protected health information to carry out their public health mission. Accordingly, the rule permits covered entities to disclose protected health information without authorization for specified public health purposes."

CLINICAL RESEARCH

Clinical research is an integral part of the healthcare industry. It allows for advances in healthcare and improved patient care. However, such advances are dependent on excellent research and proper research methodologies such as Good Clinical Research Practice (GCP). According to the WHO, GCP is a process that incorporates established ethical and scientific quality standards for the design, conduct, recording, and reporting of clinical research involving the participation of human subjects and provides public assurance that the rights, safety, and well-being of research subjects are protected.

AUTHORIZATION AND INFORMED CONSENT

In regards to clinical research an authorization is different than informed consent. An authorization is an individual's permission for a covered entity to use or disclose PHI for a specific purpose (e.g., a research study). Informed consent, on the other hand, is the individual's permission to participate in the research study. An authorization is required to contain specific elements and required statements in accordance with the Privacy Rule.

These elements and statements include:

- A description of the PHI to be used or disclosed, identifying the information in a specific and meaningful manner.
- The names or other specific identification of the person or persons (or class of persons) authorized to make the requested use or disclosure.
- The names or other specific identification of the person or persons (or class of persons) to whom the covered entity may make the requested use or disclosure.
- A description of each purpose of the requested use or disclosure.

- Authorization expiration date or expiration event that relates to the individual or to the purpose of the use or disclosure ("end of the research study" or "none" is permissible for research, including for the creation and maintenance of a research database or repository).
- Signature of the individual and date – If the individual's legally authorized representative signs the authorization, a description of the representative's authority to act for the individual must also be provided.

INSTITUTIONAL REVIEW BOARDS

All clinical research studies in the United States are reviewed by the FDA and governing bodies called institutional review boards (IRBs), whose job is to make sure participants' rights are fully protected and that participants are not exposed to any unnecessary risks. An IRB is charged with protecting the rights and welfare of people involved in research. This is accomplished by making sure critical activities and industry best practices are being followed. Although a comprehensive discussion on clinical trial best practices is outside the scope of this discussion, healthcare organizations participating in this sector must recognize that a comprehensive program that is compliant with all applicable laws and regulations must be in place when performing clinical trials.

HEALTHCARE RECORDS MANAGEMENT

Proper healthcare records management is a critical part of today's healthcare systems. As the healthcare industry strives for efficiency and automation, proper management of healthcare records becomes increasingly important. Furthermore, effective healthcare records management programs support compliance with various legal and regulatory requirements. Although each organization will need to develop a program that meets its specific needs, two essential elements are generation and maintenance of records (including quality and access control, and management and distribution) and proper destruction of healthcare records. Healthcare record information must be properly managed and safeguarded from start (record generation) to finish (record destruction) and the entire time in between. Although each organization will need to comply with specific organizational, jurisdictional, and legal/regulatory data retention requirements, there are some industry best practices that should be followed around proper data destruction. According to the HHS, the HIPAA Privacy and Security Rules offer the following guidance on proper data destruction:

"Depending on the circumstances, proper disposal methods may include (but are not limited to):

- Shredding or otherwise destroying PHI in paper records so that the PHI is rendered essentially unreadable, indecipherable, and otherwise cannot be reconstructed prior to it being placed in a dumpster or other trash receptacle.

- Maintaining PHI for disposal in a secure area and using a disposal vendor as a business associate to pick up and shred or otherwise destroy the PHI.
- In justifiable cases, based on the size and the type of the covered entity, and the nature of the PHI, depositing PHI in locked dumpsters that are accessible only by authorized persons, such as appropriate refuse workers.
- For PHI on electronic media, clearing (using software or hardware products to overwrite media with non-sensitive data), purging (degaussing or exposing the media to a strong magnetic field in order to disrupt the recorded magnetic domains), or destroying the media (disintegration, pulverization, melting, incinerating, or shredding)."

DATA SHARING

Healthcare organizations must note that under HIPAA's transaction, privacy, and security rules, when sharing protected health information, it should be properly safeguarded. Each of the HIPAA transactions, privacy, and security rules also references agreements or contracts among organizational entities. According to the American Health Information Management Association (AHIMA), "The HIPAA transactions, security, and privacy regulations identify five agreements and relationships that can be established between healthcare entities to achieve economies of scale and lessen HIPAA's administrative burden. They are:

- Affiliated covered entity (ACE)
- Business associate contract
- Chain of trust agreement
- Data use agreement
- Organized healthcare arrangement (OHCA)
- Trading partner agreement"

UNDERSTANDING EXTERNAL THIRD-PARTY RELATIONSHIPS

In order for healthcare organizations to deliver quality care, at a low cost, and efficiently, they must often work with external organizations to achieve their healthcare delivery goals. The specifics of each relationship vary among individual healthcare organizations and their selected third-party partners. If a vendor receives PHI from a healthcare organization, the vendor is considered a business partner. The term business partner is formally defined under HIPAA, and all business partners of a healthcare organization must agree in writing to certain mandatory provisions regarding the proper safeguarding, use, and disclosure of protected health information. Healthcare organizations must take note that the HIPAA Transaction Rule describes the use of a Trading Partner Agreement.

The Trading Partner Agreement specifies various technical requirements for communications protocols, such as:

- How the transactions are to be addressed
- What character set must be used
- Whether receipt will be acknowledged

Although the Transaction Rule does not require a Trading Partner Agreement, if one is used, the rule specifies what may not be included in the agreement. The Trading Partner Agreement cannot:

- Change any definition, data condition, or use of a data element
- Add any data elements or segments to the maximum defined data set
- Require use of any codes or data elements that are marked "not used" or are not present in the implementation guide
- Change the meaning or intent of the standard's implementation specification

INFORMATION FLOW AND LIFE CYCLE IN THE HEALTHCARE ENVIRONMENTS

Healthcare organizations create, receive, and distribute massive amounts of sensitive data that flow internally (e.g., within organizational boundaries and among its employees) and externally (e.g., with third-party relationships) in the delivery and management of modern healthcare services. This information flow will vary among healthcare organizations based on the type, size, and healthcare services that are delivered. There are a number of technologies and strategies that organizations can deploy to address their specific operating, business, and regulatory requirements. Although a detailed discussion is outside the scope of this book, and it is the responsibility of each individual organization to select technology solutions that meet their needs, there are some common considerations that all organizations need to consider when addressing information flow and life cycle within their specific operating environment. The common considerations often include information flow and data mapping, security and privacy issues, data quality, data management and retention, and data destruction.

HEALTH DATA CHARACTERIZATION

Since most healthcare organizations have a tremendous amount of data, much of which is PHI, they face many data management challenges on the daily basis. In order to properly protect and manage data, they should be characterized by the organization. Data characterization is best considered an umbrella term that encompasses the following:

- **Classification** – Labels similar data types into groups based on sensitivity level (e.g., confidential, public use) allowing for consistency and proper data handling across the organization.
- **Taxonomy** – Is a hierarchical organizational system that structures data into categories and subcategories. It is used to simplify vocabulary and avoid confusion since it becomes a commonly understood and agreed-upon classification.
- **Analytics** – Various scientific and mathematically based processes that can support data management in a healthcare organization.

HEALTHCARE PROVIDER TAXONOMY CODES

The National Uniform Claim Committee (NUCC) for standardized classification of healthcare providers maintains the Healthcare Provider Taxonomy Codes (HPTCs).

The NUCC updates the code set twice a year with changes effective April 1 and October 1. The CMS in partnership with the NUCC maintains the following code lists:

- **Health Care Code Lists:**
  - Claim Adjustment Reason Codes (CARC)
  - Remittance Advice Remark Codes (RARC)
  - Claim Status Category Codes
  - Claim Status Codes
  - Health Care Service Type Codes
  - Health Care Services Decision Reason Codes
  - HPTCs
  - Provider Characteristics Codes
  - Insurance Business Process Application Error Codes
- **Health Insurance Exchange Code Lists:**
  - Payment-type codes
  - Report-type codes

DATA ANALYTICS

Industry experts have not agreed upon the exact definition of data analytics. The ever-changing technology, industry-specific uses, and organizational nuances add to the challenge of a universal definition. However, most organizations agree that data analytics involves the collection, processing, and scientific or mathematical analysis of the organization's business intelligence (information generated from its systems and applications). The output of this information can be used by organizations in a variety of ways. Additionally, there are several common types of analytics and methodologies (e.g., statistical, contextual, quantitative, predictive) and a detailed review is outside the scope of this discussion. However, regardless of the definition or methodology selected, organizations find tremendous value in adopting data analytics. The adoption of such programs leads to greater efficiency, improved organizational knowledge, and increased business value. For healthcare organizations this can mean anything from the analysis of business services (e.g., how many new patients joined our service through social media recommendations) to clinical research (e.g., which medicines were most effective for treating a particular disease). It is important to note that healthcare organizations must properly safeguard any patient health information used or generated in analytics.

DATA INTEROPERABILITY AND EXCHANGE

According to the HIMSS, "Interoperability is the ability of different information technology systems and software applications to communicate, exchange data, and use the information that has been exchanged. Data exchange schema and standards should permit data to be shared across clinicians, lab, hospital, pharmacy, and patient regardless of the application or application vendor." HIMSS continues to explain that there are three levels of HIT interoperability. It defines the levels as:

- **Foundational** – Interoperability allows data exchange from one information technology system to be received by another and does not require the ability for the receiving information technology system to interpret the data.
- **Structural** – Interoperability is an intermediate level that defines the structure or format of data exchange (i.e., the message format standards) where there is uniform movement of healthcare data from one system to another such that the clinical or operational purpose and meaning of the data is preserved and unaltered. Structural interoperability defines the syntax of the data exchange. It ensures that data exchanges between information technology systems can be interpreted at the data field level.
- **Semantic** – Interoperability provides interoperability at the highest level, which is the ability of two or more systems or elements to exchange information and to use the information that has been exchanged. Semantic interoperability takes advantage of both the structuring of the data exchange and the codification of the data including vocabulary so that the receiving information technology systems can interpret the data. This level of interoperability supports the

electronic exchange of patient summary information among caregivers and other authorized parties via potentially disparate EHR systems and other systems to improve quality, safety, efficiency, and efficacy of healthcare delivery.

INTEGRATING THE HEALTHCARE ENTERPRISE

According to the Integrating the Healthcare Enterprise (IHE) website, IHE "Is an initiative by health care professionals and industry to improve the way computer systems in health care share information. IHE promotes the coordinated use of established standards such as DICOM and HL7 to address specific clinical needs in support of optimal patient care. Systems developed in accordance with IHE communicate with one another better, are easier to implement, and enable care providers to use information more effectively."

HEALTH LEVEL SEVEN INTERNATIONAL

According to the Health Level Seven International (HL7) website, "Health Level Seven International (HL7) is a not-for-profit, ANSI-accredited standards developing organization dedicated to providing a comprehensive framework and related standards for the exchange, integration, sharing, and retrieval of electronic health information that supports clinical practice and the management, delivery, and evaluation of health services." Since HL7 utilizes open system architecture, any healthcare organization adopting HL7 standards can interface with any other organization, system, or application also using HL7.

DIGITAL IMAGING AND COMMUNICATIONS IN MEDICINE (DICOM)

According to the Association of Electrical Equipment and Medical Imaging Manufacturers, DICOM is "The international standard for medical images and related information (ISO 12052). It defines the formats for medical images that can be exchanged with the data and quality necessary for clinical use. DICOM is implemented in almost every radiology, cardiology imaging, and radiotherapy device (X-ray, CT, MRI, ultrasound, etc.), and increasingly in devices in other medical domains such as ophthalmology and dentistry."

LEGAL MEDICAL RECORDS

According to the HIMSS, "Healthcare organizations across the country recognize the benefits of Electronic Health Records (EHRs) to improve care, reduce costs, and improve efficiency." However, organizations must also recognize the legal implications of the EHR. An organization's healthcare records must meet all statutory, regulatory, and professional requirements for both clinical and business purposes. HIMSS recommends, "EHR selection criteria must include ensuring that a given EHR is appropriately designed and can be appropriately used to ensure adherence to federal and state rules, as well as institutional requirements and additional certification standards that may apply to their organization." Although the specifics will vary among individual organizations, HIMSS suggests the following policy elements be included by healthcare organizations when addressing the legal elements of EHRs:

- Unique health record created and maintained for each patient
- Content requirements including author, date, time, and authentication
- Access, privacy, confidentiality, and security policies
- Policies and procedures for amendments, corrections, timeliness, completeness, and late entries
- Policies and procedures for forms, templates, and voice recognition and dictation
- Policies and procedures for records retention, records archiving and destruction, coding and abstracting, data quality management, and reporting

DEFINITIONS

Term	Definition
Affiliated Covered Entity (ACE)	Legally separate covered entities that are affiliated may designate themselves as a single covered entity for purposes of the HIPAA Privacy Rule
Ambulatory Patient Groups (APG)	Encompass a full range of ambulatory settings and designed to explain the amount and type of resources used in an ambulatory visit
Authorization	Authorization is an individual's permission for a covered entity to use or disclose PHI for a certain purpose, such as a research study
Catastrophic health insurance plan	A catastrophic health insurance plan covers essential health benefits but has a very high deductible. This means it provides a kind of "safety net" coverage in case the patient has an accident or serious illness
Chain of Trust Agreement	The Chain of Trust Agreement is described as a contract in which the parties agree to electronically exchange data and to protect the transmitted data
Covered entity	A HIPAA covered entity is any organization or corporation that directly handles personal health information (PHI) or personal health records (PHRs)

Term	Definition
Diagnosis-Related Groups (DRG)	Payment approach that focuses on inpatient hospitalizations, setting a price based on categories of illness
Digital Imaging and Communications in Medicine (DICOM)	DICOM is the international standard for medical images and related information (ISO 12052). It defines the formats for medical images that can be exchanged with the data and quality necessary for clinical use
Electronic data interchange (EDI)	Electronic data interchange
Electronic Health Records (EHR)	EHRs are electronic systems that store a patient's health information, such as the patient's history of diseases and which medications the patient is taking. They allow doctors to easily keep track of patients' health information and may enable them to access patients' information when a patient has a problem even if their doctor's office is closed
Exclusive provider organizations (EPOs)	EPOs are similar to PPOs except that patients will only be reimbursed for healthcare services provided within the network
Good Clinical Research Practice (GCP)	GCP is a process that incorporates established ethical and scientific quality standards for the design, conduct, recording, and reporting of clinical research involving the participation of human subjects. Compliance with GCP provides public assurance that the rights, safety, and well-being of research subjects are protected and respected and ensures the integrity of clinical research data
Healthcare clearinghouse	Organizations that process nonstandard data elements of health information into standard data elements
Health Information Technology (HIT)	The exchange of health information in an electronic environment
Health Level Seven International (HL7)	HL7 is a not-for-profit, ANSI-accredited standards developing organization dedicated to providing a comprehensive framework and related standards for the exchange, integration, sharing, and retrieval of electronic health information that supports clinical practice and the management, delivery, and evaluation of health services
Health Maintenance Organization (HMO)	Patient pays a set premium and is entitled services included in the benefit offering. Patients must see a primary care physician within the HMO, and are required to obtain a referral for specialists and additional healthcare services not included in the HMO's primary offering
High-deductible health plans (HDHPs)	HDHPs are plans with high deductibles, but these are balanced with very low premiums

Term	Definition
Indemnity plan	Patient selects healthcare provider of their choice. The service provider submits a claim to the patient's insurance for services rendered
Legal medical record	An organization's healthcare records must meet all statutory, regulatory, and professional requirements for both clinical and business purposes
Medicaid	U.S. government insurance program that provides insurance for the poor
Medical device	An article, instrument, apparatus, or machine that is used in the prevention, diagnosis, or treatment of illness or disease, or for detecting, measuring, restoring, correcting, or modifying the structure or function of the body for some health purpose
Medicare	U.S. government insurance program that provides insurance for the elderly
National Uniform Billing Committee (NUBC)	A voluntary committee whose work is coordinated through the offices of the American Hospital Association (AHA) and includes participation of all the major national provider and payer organizations
Payer	Refers to entities other than the patient that finance or reimburse the cost of healthcare services
Personal health records	An electronic application used by patients to maintain and manage their health information in a private, secure, and confidential environment
Point-of-service plan	A POS is a hybrid between an HMO and a PPO
Preferred provider organization (PPO)	A PPO can be considered a hybrid of an indemnity plan and an HMO. Patients can select a healthcare provider of their choice, as long as it is within PPO network. Some PPOs will allow patients to select service outside of the network, but will usually only reimburse patients for a smaller percentage than if they had stayed within the network
Reimbursement	Reimbursement is being repaid or compensated for expenses already incurred or, as in the case of healthcare, for services that have already been provided
Resource Utilization Groups (RUGs)	Each facility is paid a daily rate based on the needs of individual Medicare patients, with an adjustment for local labor cost
Taxonomy	A hierarchical organizational system that structures data into categories and subcategories. It is used to simplify vocabulary and avoid confusion since it becomes a commonly understood and agreed-upon classification

Practice Exam

1. A healthcare provider is:
   a. A provider of medical or health services in the normal course of business
   b. Synonymous with a covered entity under HIPAA
   c. Any organization or corporation that directly handles PHI
   d. None of the above
2. A covered entity is:
   a. A provider of medical or health services in the normal course of business
   b. Synonymous with a healthcare provider under HIPAA
   c. Any organization or corporation that directly handles PHI
   d. None of the above
3. EDI is:
   a. Electric data interchange
   b. Electronic dental interchange
   c. Electronic data interchange
   d. Electronic data import
4. Business associates:
   a. Provide medical services
   b. Provide support services to medical providers
   c. Are not required to comply with HIPAA
   d. Both b and c
5. HIT is an acronym for:
   a. Healthcare information technician
   b. Health information technology
   c. Healthcare information technology
   d. Health information technician
6. Medical devices are classified into:
   a. Three regulatory categories
   b. Six regulatory categories
   c. One regulatory category
   d. None of the above
7. An EHR is:
   a. An electronic health record
   b. Different from a personal health record
   c. Synonymous with a personal health record
   d. Both a and b
8. Meaningful use is:
   a. A major driver of health information technology
   b. Optional for smaller organizations
   c. Only beneficial for healthcare organizations
   d. None of the above

9. The two basic types of health insurance are:
   a. PPO and POS
   b. Medicare and Medicaid
   c. Public and private
   d. HMO and PPO

10. Healthcare coding is:
    a. Essential to the transactional aspect of healthcare delivery
    b. Required under HIPAA
    c. Only important to large healthcare organizations who use third-party billing services
    d. Both a and b

11. HCPCS is an acronym for:
    a. Healthcare Communication Procedure Coding System
    b. Healthcare Common Procedure Communication System
    c. Healthcare Common Procedure Coding System
    d. None of the above

12. SNOMED CT is an acronym for:
    a. Systematized Nomenclature of Medicine Clinical Terms
    b. Systematized Nomenclature of Medicine Clerical Terms
    c. Systematized Naming of Medical Clinical Terms
    d. None of the above

13. TCS is an acronym for:
    a. Transactions and Code Sets
    b. Technology and Code Sets
    c. Transfer and Code Sets
    d. None of the above

14. SNOWMED CT often includes:
    a. Diagnosis-Related Groups (DRGs)
    b. Ambulatory Patient Groups (APGs)
    c. Resource Utilization Groups (RUGs)
    d. All of the above

15. The National Uniform Billing Committee:
    a. Is a voluntary committee
    b. Is coordinated through the American Hospital Association
    c. Manages standards for uniform billing
    d. All of the above

16. A healthcare clearinghouse:
    a. Provides patient care
    b. Only processes Medicare and Medicaid claims
    c. Only processes private insurance claims
    d. None of the above

17. Public Health Reporting Regulations:
    a. Are addressed under HIPAA
    b. Require patient authorization
    c. Only apply to public health insurance programs
    d. None of the above
18. Health records management:
    a. Is important from beginning to end of the health record
    b. Addresses data and quality management
    c. Addresses record destruction
    d. All of the above
19. Data characterization includes:
    a. Classification
    b. Taxonomy
    c. Analytics
    d. All of the above
20. DICOM is an acronym for:
    a. Digital Imaging and Compliance in Medicine
    b. Digital Integrity and Communications in Medicine
    c. Digital Imaging and Communications in Medicine
    d. Direct Imaging and Communications in Medicine

Practice Exam Answers

1. a
2. c
3. c
4. d
5. b
6. a
7. d
8. a
9. c
10. d
11. c
12. a
13. a
14. d
15. d
16. d
17. a
18. d
19. a
20. a

References

http://www.hhs.gov/.

http://www.minnesotamedicine.com/Past-Issues/Past-Issues-2011/February-2011/Five-Payment-Models-The-Pros-the-Cons.

http://www.himss.org/library/ehr/.

http://www.healthit.gov/providers-professionals/faqs/what-personal-health-record.

https://nppes.cms.hhs.gov/NPPES/NPIRegistryHome.do.

https://www.healthcare.gov/glossary/health-insurance/.

http://www.who.int/medical_devices/definitions/en/.

http://www.fda.gov/medicaldevices/deviceregulationandguidance/overview/classifyyourdevice/default.htm.

http://www.healthit.gov/policy-researchers-implementers/meaningful-use-regulations.

http://medical-dictionary.thefreedictionary.com/payer.

http://aspe.hhs.gov/admnsimp/final/txfin00.htm.

http://www.cms.gov/Regulations-and-Guidance/HIPAA-Administrative-Simplification/TransactionCodeSetsStands/index.html?redirect=/transactioncodesetsstands/02_transaction-sandcodesetsregulations.asp.

https://www.healthcare.gov/get-covered-a-1-page-guide-to-the-health-insurance-marketplace/.

http://www.hhs.gov/ocr/privacy/hipaa/understanding/special/healthit/.

https://www.healthcare.gov/what-are-the-different-types-of-health-insurance/.

http://www.cms.gov/Medicare/Coding/MedHCPCSGenInfo/index.html?redirect=/medhcpcsgeninfo/.

http://www.who.int/classifications/icd/en/.

http://www.ama-assn.org/ama/pub/physician-resources/solutions-managing-your-practice/coding-billing-insurance/cpt/about-cpt.page?

http://www.ihtsdo.org/snomed-ct/.

http://www.cms.gov/Regulations-and-Guidance/HIPAA-Administrative-Simplification/TransactionCodeSetsStands/index.html?redirect=/transactioncodesetsstands/02_transaction-sandcodesetsregulations.asp.

http://www.x12.org/.

http://www.nubc.org/aboutus/index.dhtml.

http://www.cms.gov/Regulations-and-Guidance/HIPAA-Administrative-Simplification/HIPAAGenInfo/Downloads/CoveredEntitycharts.pdf.

http://www.hhs.gov/ocr/privacy/hipaa/understanding/special/publichealth/.

http://apps.who.int/prequal/info_general/documents/GCP/GCP_handbook.pdf.

http://www.hhs.gov/ocr/privacy/hipaa/understanding/special/research/research.pdf.

http://www.phrma.org/sites/default/files/pdf/042009_clinical_trial_principles_final.pdf.

http://www.hhs.gov/ocr/privacy/hipaa/enforcement/examples/disposalfaqs.pdf.

http://library.ahima.org/xpedio/groups/public/documents/ahima/bok1_014066.hcsp?dDocName=bok1_014066.

http://www.wpc-edi.com/reference/.

http://www.gartner.com/it-glossary/analytics/.

http://www.hl7.org/.

http://medical.nema.org/Dicom/about-DICOM.html.

http://www.himss.org/library/interoperability-standards/what-is.

http://www.ihe.net/.

http://www.hhs.gov/ocr/privacy/hipaa/administrative/securityrule/securityrulepdf.pdf.

http://www.himss.org/files/HIMSSorg/content/files/LegalEMR_Flyer3.pdf.

http://www.hhs.gov/ocr/privacy/hipaa/understanding/consumers/medicalrecords.html.

Regulatory Environment

LEGAL ISSUES THAT PERTAIN TO INFORMATION SECURITY AND PRIVACY FOR HEALTHCARE ORGANIZATIONS

Under the wide array of legal issues, healthcare organizations face several challenges around information security and privacy. In addition to there being high-level governance frameworks, many of the specific security and privacy requirements impact the operations of healthcare organizations. Although all healthcare organization employees have the responsibility for properly safeguarding healthcare information, security, and privacy, professionals are at the forefront of compliance with legal and regulatory requirements associated with healthcare delivery.

HEALTH INSURANCE PORTABILITY AND ACCOUNTABILITY ACT OF 1996 (HIPAA)

In the United States, one of the most important healthcare laws is HIPAA. According to the Office for Civil Rights, "The Office for Civil Rights enforces the HIPAA Privacy Rule, which protects the privacy of individually identifiable health information; the HIPAA Security Rule, which sets national standards for the security of electronic protected health information; the HIPAA Breach Notification Rule, which requires covered entities and business associates to

33

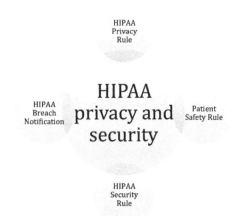

FIGURE 3.1 Elements of HIPAA.

provide notification following a breach of unsecured protected health information; and the confidentiality provisions of the Patient Safety Rule, which protect identifiable information being used to analyze patient safety events and improve patient safety." Although HIPAA contains several legislative mandates, the most relevant section to information security is the Administrative Simplification section. This section includes the standards for privacy, security, and enforcement. Figure 3.1 shows the relationship between the various elements of HIPAA.

SELECT ELEMENTS AND DEFINITIONS

As stated earlier, HIPAA has several elements and covers a number of issues that healthcare organizations must comply with. However, for exam preparation purposes we would like to highlight some select elements and definitions from HIPAA. According to the HIPAA, Public Law 104-191 (August 21, 1996), Subtitle F Administrative Simplification, Part C, Section 1171, the term "health information" means any information, whether oral or recorded in any form or medium, that:

1. Is created or received by a health care provider, health plan, public health authority, employer, life insurer, school or university, or health care clearinghouse; and
2. Relates to the past, present, or future physical or mental health or condition of an individual; the provision of health care to an individual; or the past, present, or future payment for the provision of health care to an individual.

Individually identifiable health information is information that is a subset of health information, including demographic information collected from an individual, and:

1. Is created or received by a health care provider, health plan, employer, or health care clearinghouse; and
2. Relates to the past, present, or future physical or mental health or condition of an individual; the provision of health care to an individual; or the past, present, or future payment for the provision of health care to an individual; and:
   a. That identifies the individual; or
   b. With respect to which there is a reasonable basis to believe the information can be used to identify the individual.

Additionally, protected health information is defined by 45 CFR 160.103, and, as defined, is referenced in Section 13400 of Subtitle D ("Privacy") of the Health Information Technology for Economic and Clinical Health Act (HITECH Act).

"Protected health information means individually identifiable health information [defined above]:

(1) Except as provided in paragraph
(2) of this definition, that is:
    (i) Transmitted by electronic media;
    (ii) Maintained in electronic media; or
    (iii) Transmitted or maintained in any other form or medium.
(2) Protected health information excludes individually identifiable health information in:
    (i) Education records covered by the Family Educational Rights and Privacy Act, as amended, 20 U.S.C. 1232g;
    (ii) Records described at 20 U.S.C. 1232g(a)(4)(B)(iv); and
    (iii) Employment records held by a covered entity in its role as employer."

THE AMERICAN RECOVERY AND REINVESTMENT ACT (ARRA) OF 2009

The ARRA of 2009 was enacted to provide stimulus and recovery mechanisms in response to the great recession. Although there are many elements to ARRA, most of which are outside the scope of this book, we focus our discussions on select healthcare domains, specifically the HITECH Act and amendments to HIPAA.

The most significant changes to HIPAA now include:

- The final Breach Notification Rule
- Updates to business associate responsibilities

FIGURE 3.2 Relationship between HITECH and HIPAA.

- Expansion of the penalty consequences
- Investigative authority for potential violations to the Attorney General of each state

With these changes to HIPAA, healthcare organizations were required to expand and enforce their own privacy and security structures as well as expand the controls to their business relationships and partners with whom they share healthcare information.

According to the Office for Civil Rights, "The Health Information Technology for Economic and Clinical Health (HITECH) Act, enacted as part of the American Recovery and Reinvestment Act of 2009, was signed into law on February 17, 2009, to promote the adoption and meaningful use of health information technology. Subtitle D of the HITECH Act addresses the privacy and security concerns associated with the electronic transmission of health information, in part, through several provisions that strengthen the civil and criminal enforcement of the HIPAA rules." Figure 3.2 demonstrates the relationship between HITECH Act and HIPAA privacy and security rules. Specifically, they work together to ensure privacy and security concerns are properly addressed as healthcare organizations adopt and extend the meaningful use of health information technology (IT).

INTERNATIONAL STANDARDS

When looking outside of U.S. boundaries, many international healthcare organizations face similar legal and regulatory challenges. Several countries are developing or adhering to regulations that require the protection of personally identifiable information used by healthcare organizations. Some of the more common laws and regulations include:

- **Canada's Personal Information Protection and Electronic Documents Act (PIPEDA)** – Sets out ground rules for how private sector organizations may collect, use, or disclose personal information in the course of commercial activities.

- **European Commission Data Protection Legislation** – Various legislation, documents, and guidance on the protection of personal data within the European Union.
- **UK Data Protection Act 1998** – Controls how organizations, businesses, or the government uses your personal information.

A CULTURE OF PRIVACY AND SECURITY

It is important to remember that employees take their cues from the organization's senior leadership. When senior leaders place importance on proactive security and privacy programs, healthcare organizations can properly safeguard the personal health information (PHI) entrusted to them by the patients they serve. This "tone at the top" not only enables the right attitude when delivering patient care services but also ensures that privacy and security professionals have the resources they need. Although it is important to remember that every employee at a healthcare organization is responsible for safeguarding PHI, privacy and security professionals are charged with the protection of PHI on a daily basis. Although there can be subtle differences between the specific roles of privacy and security professionals, we think it is best to focus on the intent and key principles needed to support effective privacy and security programs and leave organizational structure and job roles to be managed by individual healthcare organizations. Both privacy and security efforts should be thoroughly documented in policies, procedures, and standards within the organization. Additionally, those efforts need to be supported by the organization's senior leadership.

ORGANIZATIONAL-LEVEL PRIVACY AND SECURITY REQUIREMENTS

Many organizations find it is best to focus on the successful implementation and management of comprehensive privacy and security programs based on industry best practices. A majority of the time, doing so complies with most specific regulatory or legal requirements and provides greater program efficiency as opposed to chasing various fragmented regulatory requirements as disparate compliance activities. Some of the key privacy and security principles organizations should focus on include the following:

- The PHI must be collected by an organization for a specific purpose and used only for that purpose.
- PHI must be kept isolated from any persons who are not authorized by the organization or the original data owner.
- The information must be deleted at an appropriate time (i.e., when no longer needed for its intended purpose).

DATA BREACH REGULATIONS

Unfortunately, even with all of a healthcare organization's privacy and security controls in place, there is a good chance a data breach will occur. Organizations are obligated to take certain steps when a data breach has been believed to occur. Understanding the definition of a data breach and the required steps after a breach is critical for healthcare organizations. This knowledge and understanding enables compliance with various regulatory and legal requirements. According to the U.S. Health and Human Services Office for Civil Rights, "A breach is, generally, an impermissible use or disclosure under the Privacy Rule that compromises the security or privacy of the protected health information. An impermissible use or disclosure of protected health information is presumed to be a breach unless the covered entity or business associate, as applicable, demonstrates that there is a low probability that the protected health information has been compromised based on a risk assessment of at least the following factors:

1. The nature and extent of the protected health information involved, including the types of identifiers and the likelihood of re-identification;
2. The unauthorized person who used the protected health information or to whom the disclosure was made;
3. Whether the protected health information was actually acquired or viewed; and
4. The extent to which the risk to the protected health information has been mitigated."

In addition to understanding how data breaches are defined, healthcare organizations must also understand their reporting responsibilities. Specifically, the Office for Civil Rights declares that "The HIPAA Breach Notification Rule, 45 CFR §§ 164.400-414, requires HIPAA covered entities and their business associates to provide notification following a breach of unsecured protected health information. Similar breach notification provisions implemented and enforced by the Federal Trade Commission apply to vendors of personal health records and their third party service providers, pursuant to section 13407 of the HITECH Act." From an operational perspective, this means that organizations must have policies and procedures in place to detect and respond to data breaches and have the capabilities for proper notification in accordance with industry best practices and in adherence with legal and regulatory requirements.

PENALTIES AND FEES

Healthcare organizations should not only focus on proactive measures to avoid privacy and security problems but also need to understand the consequences of not having effective privacy and security programs and noncompliance with regulatory requirements. Many legal and regulatory requirements have specific penalties and fines for noncompliance. One stringent example

TABLE 1—CATEGORIES OF VIOLATIONS AND RESPECTIVE PENALTY AMOUNTS AVAILABLE

Violation category—Section 1176(a)(1)	Each violation	All such violations of an identical provision in a calendar year
(A) Did Not Know	$100–$50,000	$1,500,000
(B) Reasonable Cause	1,000–50,000	1,500,000
(C)(i) Willful Neglect—Corrected	10,000–50,000	1,500,000
(C)(ii) Willful Neglect—Not Corrected	50,000	1,500,000

FIGURE 3.3 HIPAA violation and corresponding penalties.

is ARRA of 2009, which included updates to HIPAA and increased the penalties for unauthorized disclosure of PHI. Fines can be levied up to $1.5 million per annum. Figure 3.3 from the Federal Register (Vol. 74, No. 209, Friday, October 30, 2009) depicts the specific penalties.

45 CFR 164.514: HIPAA PRIVACY RULE (THE DE-IDENTIFICATION STANDARD AND ITS TWO IMPLEMENTATION SPECIFICATIONS)

As part of understanding and complying with the HIPAA Privacy Rule, careful consideration must be given to data de-identification and the associated implementation specifications. The focus of this chapter is on the healthcare regulatory environment and at this point in the exam preparation process, it is only important to note that there are 18 personal data identifiers and the standard requires that data be de-identified following the 2-implementation specifications. Additional, specific information on the 18 personal data identifiers and the implementation standards are discussed in Chapter 4.

In common practice, the list of the 18 personal data identifiers helps organizations understand that if a document or set of information contains any of these characteristics or combinations of personal data identifiers, about an individual or a number of individuals, then that set of information should be considered PHI and protected accordingly.

INFORMATION FLOW MAPPING

Given the inordinate and ever-growing amount of data most healthcare organizations have in their possession, managing data and information flows is of the utmost importance. This often proves to be challenging for many healthcare organizations given the volume and types of data within their environment. Specifically, organizations need to determine what data are considered PHI and where they are located on their infrastructure, which commonly includes servers, storage, and endpoint devices. Unfortunately, many data breaches occur when organizations do not properly identify the entire range of PHI that flows through their environment and therefore cannot implement the appropriate safeguards. Ignorance of where PHI is located within an organization's boundaries does not exonerate the organization from legal and regulatory compliance. This is why information flow mapping is critical to healthcare organizations protecting PHI in their possession.

MONITORING PHI INFORMATION FLOWS

After a healthcare organization identifies PHI and implements appropriate safeguards, they must also continuously monitor the information flow and access to the information, and report any breaches if the information is inappropriately accessed or otherwise compromised. For many organizations this means the need to institute information security practices and associated technology that can identify and protect the stored PHI, control access to the PHI, and manage the information flow inside and outside the organization's physical, logical, and legal boundaries.

JURISDICTIONAL IMPLICATIONS

In addition to organizations needing to understand the relationship that PHI has within their physical, logical, and legal boundaries, they must also be aware of any jurisdictional issues. Healthcare organizations in today's digitally connected world have many external, but interconnected business relationships associated with their healthcare delivery services. This requires healthcare organizations to be aware of any data sharing issues, particularly when transacting with other organizations across local, state, national, or international boundaries. Understanding the jurisdictional implications of sharing data from one organization to another ahead of time is essential so that each organization can understand any liabilities and responsibilities involved in the exchange of healthcare information. However, understanding is just the first step, and healthcare entities must implement the appropriate privacy and safeguards.

DATA USE AND RECIPROCAL SUPPORT AGREEMENT (DURSA)

The DURSA is a common data sharing agreement that enables healthcare organizations to share information. Prior to the development of DURSA, many organizations struggled with sharing information due to the lack of uniform standards across various state and local healthcare privacy and security laws. The Office of the National Coordinator for Health IT developed the DURSA for organizations participating in electronic health information exchanges (HIEs). It was built upon the legal requirements of the participants and seeks to provide a framework that insures protection for health information during exchanges. The Agreement reflects consensus among the state-level, federal-level, and private entities regarding the following issues:

- Multiparty agreement
- Participants actively engaged in HIE
- Privacy and security obligations
- Requests for information based on a permitted purpose
- Duty to respond
- Future use of data received from another participant
- Respective duties of submitting and receiving participants
- Autonomy principle for access
- Use of authorizations to support requests for data
- Participant breach notification
- Mandatory nonbinding dispute resolution
- Allocation of liability risk

DATA SUBJECTS

The specific data elements of human subjects commonly contained in PHI entrusted to healthcare organizations are extremely valuable. These data have tremendous value on the black market and are therefore highly valued and targeted by cybercriminals. With the ubiquitous nature of today's PHI being made available electronically, organizations find themselves as primary targets and face an ever-increasing amount of cyber attacks.

DATA OWNERSHIP

Although a patient is the ultimate owner of their personal healthcare information, there are many individuals (e.g., controllers, custodians, processors) within a healthcare organization who collectively have responsibilities for protecting PHI and act on the owner's behalf. Any sharing of PHI that is in possession of a healthcare organization must be done with appropriate consent. Additionally, even if the patient is not currently receiving treatment or is otherwise a current patient of the provider, the healthcare organization is still responsible for safeguarding the PHI.

LEGISLATIVE AND REGULATORY UPDATES

Since the legal and regulatory environments are constantly changing with various updates to address constant changes in society, technology, and healthcare, organizations must stay abreast of changes and revise their policies, procedures, and operations to remain compliant and in good standing. It is important to know that organizations are also responsible for providing training and awareness on said changes to ensure that all of the employees are compliant with the most up-to-date legal and regulatory requirements when delivering healthcare.

TREATIES

With an increase in globalization, countries are often compelled by businesses and healthcare organizations to find ways to conduct business despite country-specific legal and regulatory requirements. To accomplish such undertakings, countries collaborate on international agreements to address any of the differences in how PHI is used and protected. Additionally, there are many country-specific requirements, and sometimes organizations will create legal agreements that exclusively govern the partnerships and exchanges between two specific organizations. Therefore, it is best for each organization to be aware of their specific requirements and create agreements accordingly. However, there are other instances where healthcare organizations need to be aware of broader privacy and security agreements, such as Safe Harbor.

International Safe Harbor Principles

The U.S.–EU Safe Harbor is an agreed-upon process that enables U.S. companies to comply with the EU Directive 95/46/EC (the protection of personal data). Organizations operating in the European Union cannot send personal data outside of the European Economic Area (EEA) unless the organizations outside of the EEA are compliant with the Safe Harbor Privacy Principles. The seven privacy principles include:

- **Notice** – Organizations must notify individuals about the purposes for the data collection.
- **Choice** – Organizations must give individuals the opportunity to choose (i.e., opt out and opt in – an affirmative choice is required when dealing with sensitive data) if their information is to be shared with a third party or used for purposes other than it was originally collected for.
- **Onward transfer (transfers to third parties)** – Prior to transfer organizations must follow the principles of notice and choice.
- **Access** – Individuals must have access to personal information about them that an organization holds and be able to correct, amend, or delete that information where it is inaccurate.
- **Security** – Organizations must take reasonable precautions to protect personal information from loss, misuse, and unauthorized access, disclosure, alteration, and destruction.
- **Data integrity** – An organization should take reasonable steps to ensure that data are reliable for their intended use, accurate, complete, and current.
- **Enforcement** – There must be (a) readily available and affordable independent recourse mechanisms so that each individual's complaints and disputes can be investigated and resolved and damages awarded

where the applicable law or private sector initiatives so provide; (b) procedures for verifying that the commitments companies make to adhere to the Safe Harbor principles have been implemented; and (c) obligations to remedy problems arising out of a failure to comply with the principles.

INDUSTRY-SPECIFIC LAWS

There are several industry-specific laws and regulations that may also be applicable to a healthcare organization; many are out of scope for this discussion and preparation for the HCISPP preparation. However, the following section will review some of the more common compliance requirements facing today's organizations. Having a basic familiarity of similar legal and privacy requirements facing most organizations is beneficial to healthcare organizations, particularly when considering their scope of compliance and ensuring safeguards can be applied to other compliance requirements. However, we recommend that each organization take the time to consider any additional laws at the local, state, or federal level that may be relevant to an organization's specific business and operations models. Although not exhaustive, the following list highlights some of the more common legal and regulatory requirements facing today's healthcare organizations beyond healthcare-specific regulatory requirements:

- **Occupational Safety and Health Act of 1970 (OSH Act)** – Under the OSH Act, employers are responsible for providing a safe and healthful workplace.
- **Payment Card Industry Data Security Standards (PCI DSS)** – Provides an actionable framework for developing a robust payment card data security process, including prevention, detection, and appropriate reaction to security incidents.
- **Sarbanes–Oxley Act (SOX)** – The Act mandated a number of reforms to enhance corporate responsibility, enhance financial disclosures, and combat corporate and accounting fraud, and created the Public Company Accounting Oversight Board.

POLICIES, PROCEDURES, STANDARDS, AND GUIDELINES

At the surface, policies, procedures, standards, and guidelines sound synonymous. However, there are distinct differences and organizations must understand these subtleties as well as manage the relationship among these governance tools in order to ensure a successful privacy and security program within a healthcare organization. In Figure 3.4 is given the relationship between each distinct governance document (e.g., policy, procedure).

FIGURE 3.4 Relationship between policies, procedures, standards, and guidelines.

Now that we understand the relationship between policies, standards, and guidelines and how they support an organization's privacy and security program, we can examine the specifics of each.

Policies

Policies are high-level formal documents that briefly state the organization's perspective on a particular topic. Typically these are approved by senior management and help enforce the "tone at the top" for the organization. Since they are written at a high level, they focus on organizational objectives, rather than specific guidance on how to achieve said objectives.

Procedures

Procedures are the detailed sequential steps that are documented and inform the healthcare organization's employees on how to perform specific actions. Since policies are written at a high level and only state what the organization is trying to accomplish, procedures are needed to tell employees how to specifically accomplish the organizational objectives.

Standards

A standard is a set of specifications that must be followed by the healthcare organization's employees and typically addresses a system or technical configuration. For example, the organization might have a standard for all employee laptops using the Microsoft Windows operating system. This would specify how the operating system and laptop are configured throughout the entire organization. Standards enable organizations to have consistency. Having organizational consistency supports policies and ensures that privacy and security objectives are achieved uniformly within the organization. Standards are not optional and are required throughout the organization.

Guidelines

Guidelines are documented recommendations or suggestions that offer topic-specific guidance based on industry best practices. Most healthcare organizations

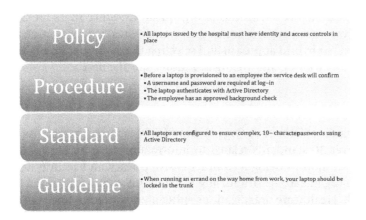

Policy
- All laptops issued by the hospital must have identity and access controls in place

Procedure
- Before a laptop is provisioned to an employee the service desk will confirm
  - A username and password are required at log–in
  - The laptop authenticates with Active Directory
  - The employee has an approved background check

Standard
- All laptops are configured to ensure complex, 10– charactepasswords using Active Directory

Guideline
- When running an errand on the way home from work, your laptop should be locked in the trunk

FIGURE 3.5 A practical example of a policy, procedure, standard, and guideline.

provide guidelines to employees to help them make reasonable choices and guide them toward decisions and producing outcomes that align with industry best practices.

A Practical Example

The following scenario can be used to exemplify the relationship between a policy, procedure, standard, and guideline. The senior leadership team at a healthcare organization is concerned about restricting access to PHI and preventing unauthorized users from accessing PHI from the organization's laptops. The senior leadership team recognizes that they need to provide information on ensuring this objective is met and know that many end users will require specific information on how to comply with the objective. Also, they recognize the controls will be more successful and easier to manage when deployed consistently across the organization. Figure 3.5 demonstrates how the earlier scenario flows across an organization's policies, procedures, standards, and guidelines.

COMMON SECURITY AND PRIVACY COMPLIANCE FRAMEWORKS

There are a number of security and privacy compliance frameworks available to healthcare organizations that can be used to ensure PHI is properly safeguarded and organizations are compliant with privacy and security, legal, and regulatory requirements. Each organization must decide which framework best suits their specific business and regulatory requirements, but the following is a list and brief description of the most common security and privacy compliance frameworks available to healthcare organizations. Since there are advantages and disadvantages between the various frameworks, we recommend taking a "best-breed" or hybrid approach and selecting the combination of frameworks that best suits your healthcare organization's specific needs.

ISO

The International Standards Organization (ISO) is recognized across the world and has over 30 standards related to information security best practices and audit. In addition to being a comprehensive privacy and security framework, healthcare organizations conducting business internationally often select this framework. Healthcare organizations either are required or find it to be a well-respected common ground by their international partners.

NATIONAL INSTITUTE OF STANDARDS AND TECHNOLOGY (NIST)

Similar to the ISO, the NIST provides a comprehensive list of standards. The most significant difference between ISO and NIST is that ISO targets the international community, while NIST is U.S. centric. The NIST Special Publication (SP) 800 series are most relevant to privacy and security. While focused on the federal government, they are free to use and can be applied to the private sector. One of the most useful SPs for healthcare organizations is SP 800-66. SP 800-66, *An Introductory Resource Guide for Implementing the Health Insurance Portability and Accountability Act (HIPAA) Security Rule*, is an invaluable resource for healthcare organizations concerned with the HIPAA Security Rule.

The remainder of the SPs offer suite of comprehensive privacy and security-related guidance. The NIST SPs can be used individually to address specific technology and security issues, but are also designed to work in conjunction (many of the documents reference other documents) so that an organization can accomplish all of its privacy and security goals within a single framework. Although the range of coverage is broad reaching, many healthcare organizations will benefit from the more commonly used documents that address areas such as encryption, security controls, risk management, and awareness and training.

NIST INTERAGENCY REPORTS (IRS)

Another important resource for healthcare organizations that is provided by NIST is the NIST IRs. The NIST IRs are research reports that provide detailed technical information on a specific topic. Healthcare organizations involved in HIEs should review the IR on the secure exchange of health information:

- NISTIR 7497 – *Security Architecture Design Process for Health Information Exchanges (HIEs)*

COMMON CRITERIA

Another widely accepted framework is the Common Criteria. According to the official Common Criteria Arrangement, "The purpose of this Arrangement is to advance those objectives by bringing about a situation in which IT products and protection profiles which earn a Common Criteria certificate can be procured or used without the need for further evaluation." They also state that the participants in the arrangement share the following objectives:

1. To ensure that evaluations of IT products and protection profiles are performed to high and consistent standards and are seen to contribute significantly to confidence in the security of those products and profiles;
2. To improve the availability of evaluated, security-enhanced IT products and protection profiles;
3. To eliminate the burden of duplicating evaluations of IT products and protection profiles;
4. To continuously improve the efficiency and cost-effectiveness of the evaluation and certification/validation process for IT products and protection profiles.

It is important to note that the Common Criteria is formally known as Common Criteria for Information Technology Security Evaluation (CC). It works with the Common Methodology for Information Technology Security Evaluation (CEM). When organizations adhere to the CC and CEM, they are well positioned to work with another organization under an internationally recognized framework. Specifically, the Common Criteria Recognition Arrangement (CCRA) manages this partnership and framework. The CCRA provides the technical basis for an international agreement among member countries. The standards and the operating methodology are based on the agreement among participating members. It is also important to note that the Common Criteria includes three distinct sets of documentation including the general model, the security functional requirements, and the security assurance requirements. This is further supported by the CEM, which describes the activities performed by an evaluator assessing the implementation of the functional and assurance requirements.

COMMON CRITERIA-CERTIFIED PRODUCT CATEGORIES

The Common Criteria certifies products under the following categories, to assist participating organizations in their selection process:

- Access control devices and systems
- Biometric systems and devices
- Boundary protection devices and systems
- Data protection

- Databases
- Detection devices and systems
- ID cards, smart cards, and smart card–related devices and systems
- Key management systems
- Multifunction devices
- Network and network-related devices and systems
- Operating systems
- Products for digital signatures
- Trusted computing

THE INFORMATION GOVERNANCE (IG) TOOLKIT

The IG Toolkit is an online self-assessment tool that enables the National Health Service (NHS) organizations and partners in the United Kingdom to comply with the Department of Health Information Governance policies and standards.

Although there are different standards for different types of organizations, the IG Toolkit assesses all organizations against the following governance requirements:

- Management structures and responsibilities (e.g., assigning responsibility for carrying out the IG assessment, providing staff training)
- Confidentiality and data protection
- Information security

GENERALLY ACCEPTED PRIVACY PRINCIPLES (GAPP)

The GAPP is a set of privacy principles that are jointly defined by the American Institute of Certified Public Accountants (AICPA) and the Canadian Institute of Chartered Accountants (CICA). The principles are based on commonly accepted privacy standards for protecting personal information. Further discussion and additional details of GAPP are in Chapter 4.

HEALTH INFORMATION TRUST ALLIANCE (HITRUST)

According to HITRUST, "The Health Information Trust Alliance (HITRUST) was born out of the belief that information security should be a core pillar of, rather than an obstacle to, the broad adoption of health information systems and exchanges."

HITRUST bases its program on the Common Security Framework (CSF). The CSF can be used by any and all organizations that create, access, store, or exchange personal health and financial information. One of the benefits of the CSF is that it was designed to align with many existing requirements. HITRUST states, "The CSF is an information security framework that harmonizes the requirements of existing standards and regulations, including federal (HIPAA, HITECH), third party (PCI, COBIT) and government (NIST, FTC)."

SANS CRITICAL SECURITY CONTROLS

The SANS 20 Critical Security Controls are essentially a subset of the NIST SP 800-53 Controls. They are a selection of the 20 most critical controls that organizations "must have in place." They are viewed as "must haves" because they are the most critical and broad-reaching controls that, when implemented correctly, provide the most value for organizations with the fewest number of control implementations. We do not advocate limiting your organization's security control framework to only 20 controls, but agree this is a great starting point, with fundamental security controls, covering a broad area of security risk. Organizations may use the SANS 20 Critical Security Controls under the Creative Commons Attribution-NoDerivs 3.0 Unported License. In accordance with the license (http://www.sans.org/critical-security-controls/) Figure 3.6 displays the latest version of the SANS 20 Critical Security Controls.

Critical Security Controls – Version 5

1. Inventory of Authorized and Unauthorized Devices
2. Inventory of Authorized and Unauthorized Software
3. Secure Configurations for Hardware and Software on Mobile Devices, Laptops, Workstations, and Servers
4. Continuous Vulnerability Assessment and Remediation
5. Malware Defenses
6. Application Software Security
7. Wireless Access Control
8. Data Recovery Capability
9. Security Skills Assessment and Appropriate Training to Fill Gaps
10. Secure Configurations for Network Devices such as Firewalls, Routers, and Switches
11. Limitation and Control of Network Ports, Protocols, and Services
12. Controlled Use of Administrative Privileges
13. Boundary Defense
14. Maintenance, Monitoring, and Analysis of Audit Logs
15. Controlled Access Based on the Need to Know
16. Account Monitoring and Control
17. Data Protection
18. Incident Response and Management
19. Secure Network Engineering
20. Penetration Tests and Red Team Exercises

FIGURE 3.6 SANS Critical Security Controls – Version 5.

RISK-BASED DECISION MAKING

Although Chapter 5 will detail specific risk management methodologies and life cycles for healthcare organizations, a brief discussion on risk-based decision making is warranted in our discussion of the regulatory environment. At a high level, the outcome of risk management activities for organizations is identifying a risk, implementing appropriate controls to reduce the identified risk, and managing any residual risk so that the organizations can achieve their business and organizational-level goals and objectives. Since there is no such thing as zero risk, healthcare organizations must take a risk-based approach and balance the identified risks against the rewards of business and financial objectives when delivering healthcare services. Figure 3.7 demonstrates the cost–benefit perspective organizations must consider when delivering today's information-based healthcare services.

We are not advocating that healthcare organizations are reckless with PHI when achieving financial and business goals. In fact, we are taking the opposite perspective. The following discussions on compensating controls and managing residual risk will allow organizations to properly safeguard PHI while balancing the business benefits with identified risks when delivering technology-based healthcare services.

COMPENSATING CONTROLS

In Chapter 4, we will detail specific types of controls that organizations can use to safeguard PHI. From a high-level perspective a control is implemented by an organization to address an identified vulnerability or risk that could be exploited by a threat. Healthcare organizations should implement a comprehensive set of primary controls to address any risks identified in their governance and risk management process. Fundamentally, there are three categories of controls (administrative, technical, and physical) with three possible implementation types (preventive, detective, and corrective) that can be applied to each category. For example, a healthcare organization can have a series of technical controls that are implemented with an end result of a preventive technical control, a detective technical control, and a corrective technical control. There is no

Business
value

Residual
risk

FIGURE 3.7 Balance of risk versus reward when delivering information-based healthcare.

limit on the combination of categories or implementation types a healthcare organization can have, but the organization must have a comprehensive and layered set of controls that addresses any identified risks. To better understand the possible range of combinations, types, and implementations available to healthcare organizations, each control category and implementation type is defined as follows:

- **Administrative** – A senior management–driven control, such as policy.
- **Logical** – System software–level control that limits access, such as role-based access controls.
- **Physical** – Provides access control at a physical layer, such as door locks.
- **Preventative** – Prevents a threat from exploiting vulnerabilities, such as a firewall.
- **Detective** – Alerts the organization that an unauthorized activity has occurred, such as an intrusion detection system.
- **Corrective** – Corrects or reduces the harmful activity from further exploiting the vulnerability, such as a patch management tool that fixes identified system issues.

Figure 3.8 displays the relationship between the three control categories (administrative, technical, and physical) and the implementation types (preventive, detective, and corrective) typically included in a set of comprehensive primary controls.

According to SANS, "Compensating controls are alternate controls designed to accomplish the intent of the original controls as closely as possible, when the originally designed controls can not be used due to limitations of the environment. These are generally required when our activity phase controls are not available or when they fail." After an organization implements their primary comprehensive control framework, other controls may be needed to address any residual risk, control failures, and gaps. Compensating controls should be implemented by healthcare organizations to address any primary control failures or shortcomings. They should be used to address any residual risk after primary controls have been implemented. Compensating controls can also allow a healthcare organization an additional layer of protection and support a defense-in-depth approach to privacy and security.

FIGURE 3.8 Relationship between control categories and implementation types.

CONTROL VARIANCE DOCUMENTATION

In a majority of circumstances healthcare organizations should be adhering to the security and privacy controls outlined in their selected framework. However, there are times where it makes sense to deviate from program specifics. Organizations must do so by leveraging a risk-based approach. These types of operational deviations should not be considered lightly or approached haphazardly. Prior to being in an actual situation that requires an operational variance to the privacy and security program, organizations must have a specific process in place that allows them to deviate from the standard program. This must occur in a controlled manner, but still accomplish the overall privacy and security goals. Most organizations will find this is best achieved by having a formal risk management and documentation process. This should be in place and designed to address operational variances, emergencies, and other unplanned events. When organizations properly document action plans and strategies ahead of an actual event, they are better prepared to deal with the situation at hand. Even with a proactive process and documentation, there still may be operational challenges, unintended consequences, and residual risk. However, if the process is comprehensive in nature and deviations are properly documented, organizations will be positioned to successfully deviate from their primary security and privacy programs, while addressing special circumstances or unplanned events. Another benefit of the documentation is that it can be used for a retrospective and organizational lessons learned. Often, during an unplanned event, organizations are consumed by managing the event at a tactical level. After the event, healthcare organizations can take a strategic perspective, and implement any required program changes identified during the retrospective. These changes can be used to enhance the existing privacy and security program.

RESIDUAL RISK TOLERANCE

As we have already stated there is no such thing as zero risk. Organizations must accept a certain level of residual risk (after implementing a comprehensive set of security controls to address the initial risk that has been identified) when delivering information-driven healthcare services. Since each healthcare organization's senior leadership team has a different level of risk acceptance, residual risk tolerance will vary greatly among organizations. Therefore, each organization must carefully consider their culture, business model, and the types of healthcare services they deliver. Although the specific business and operating requirements vary significantly among healthcare organizations, there are some common elements that impact the acceptance of residual risk. These typically include cost considerations, the regulatory environment, and technology and resource limitations. Since healthcare organizations constantly face an ever-changing threat landscape, they must continuously review their risk management programs. When doing so, they must also ensure the residual risk they accept is appropriate for the healthcare services they deliver. Finally, it is important that the senior leadership team fully understands and is accountable for the residual risk they have accepted on behalf of the organization and healthcare recipients.

ORGANIZATIONAL CODE OF ETHICS

A healthcare organization that is in possession of PHI has an ethical duty to properly safeguard PHI and associated sensitive data. Healthcare organizations are in a position of trust and the recipients of their services demand the highest ethical standards when entrusting their most personal information to a healthcare organization. Since organizations have access to the vast amounts of PHI, it is important that all employees embrace ethical behavior. Additionally senior managers must lead by example and with an ethical "tone at the top." An import step toward creating an ethical culture is for healthcare organizations to have policies, procedures, standards, training, and awareness that document and communicate the organization's Code of Ethics.

(ISC)² CODE OF ETHICS

Since the HCISPP is sponsored by the (ISC)², there is expectation that all members and certificate holders adhere to the highest level of professional standards and ethics. Specifically, the (ISC)² has a Code of Ethics that must be followed.

Code
The (ISC)² Code states the following:

"All information systems security professionals who are certified by (ISC)² recognize that such certification is a privilege that must be both earned and maintained. In support of this principle, all (ISC)² members are required to commit to fully support this Code of Ethics (the "Code"). (ISC)² members who intentionally or knowingly violate any provision of the Code will be subject to action by a peer review panel, which may result in the revocation of certification. (ISC)² members are obligated to follow the ethics complaint procedure upon observing any action by an (ISC)² member that breaches the Code. Failure to do so may be considered a breach of the Code pursuant to Canon IV.

There are only four mandatory canons in the Code. By necessity, such high-level guidance is not intended to be a substitute for the ethical judgment of the professional."

Code of Ethics Preamble

(ISC)^2 states the following for their Code of Ethics Preamble:

- "The safety and welfare of society and the common good, duty to our principals and to each other, requires that we adhere, and be seen to adhere, to the highest ethical standards of behavior.
- Therefore, strict adherence to this Code is a condition of certification."

Code of Ethics cannons

The (ISC)^2 contains the following mandatory canons in the Code:

- "Protect society, the common good, necessary public trust and confidence, and the infrastructure.
- Act honorably, honestly, justly, responsibly, and legally.
- Provide diligent and competent service to principals.
- Advance and protect the profession."

SANCTIONS

(ISC)^2 has a formal set of complaint procedures for members to address concerns of potentially unethical behavior of any member or certification holder. The procedures enable a process for reporting observations, while assuring appropriate levels of confidentiality. This includes the protection of identity from the general public of the reporting individual and the individual involved in the questionable behavior or practices. Additionally, the (ISC)^2 Board of Directors has appointed an Ethics Committee to hear all ethics complaints and make recommendations to the board. The board has final decision-making authority and the ability to provide disciplinary actions for confirmed ethical violations.

DEFINITIONS

Term	Definition
Breach	An impermissible use or disclosure under the Privacy Rule that compromises the security or privacy of the protected health information
Common Criteria	An internationally recognized technical evaluation and standards program. It is governed by agreement among member countries, using the Common Criteria Recognition Arrangement (CCRA)

Term	Definition
Compensating controls	The additional controls that can be implemented to address any primary control failures, shortcomings, or residual risk
Data controller	The senior person in charge of managing the data systems used in capturing, storing, or analyzing the PHI of patients under care of the organization. They have the responsibility for authorizing access of internal and external workforce members to the data system and its included PHI
Data custodian	The staff responsible for the maintenance and integrity of the data system – software and hardware – that houses and processes data containing PHI. This will include keeping the systems updated, backing up stored data, and maintaining and monitoring network activity for potential vulnerabilities
Data owner(s)	Two types: 1. The person to whom the actual data pertain, i.e., the patient receiving treatment for which the record is being created. This is the individual who has the final determination for how the data are used and by whom the data can be used or disclosed 2. The healthcare organization that provides the treatment services for the patient and captures information during treatment services has an ownership of the health record for the legally specified time period after the treatment has ended
Data processors	Staff who are involved in implementing the software systems that support health information processing on behalf of the data controller
Guidelines	Provide suggestions for organizational desired outcomes that align with industry best practices
Health information	The data collected about a specific person potentially across a number of treatment services from a number of healthcare organizations
Health Insurance Portability and Accountability Act of 1996 (HIPAA)	HIPAA is the federal Health Insurance Portability and Accountability Act of 1996. The primary goal of the law is to make it easier for people to keep health insurance, protect the confidentiality and security of healthcare information, and help the healthcare industry control administrative costs
Health record	The collection of health information based on treatment services provided by a healthcare organization on behalf of a patient receiving the services at that organization
IG Toolkit	A set of self-assessment steps to enable UK healthcare organizations to comply with the Department of Health Information Governance policies and standards
ISO	The International Standards Organization (ISO) is recognized across the world and has over 30 standards related to information security best practices and audit

Term	Definition
NIST	National Institute of Standards and Technology (NIST) addresses the measurement infrastructure within science and technology efforts for the U.S. federal government
Occupational Safety and Health Administration (OSHA)	A unit of the U.S. Department of Labor and addresses safety and protection of workers in organizations that involve hazards and hazardous wastes as potential sources of injuries and health-related problems
Personally identifiable information (PII)	Any information that allows positive identification of an individual, usually as a combination of several characteristics
Personal health information (PHI)	The PII involved with the healthcare and treatment of an individual
Policies	The high-level formal documents that briefly state the organization's perspective and are driven by senior management to set a "tone at the top" for the organization
Primary control	The initial set of controls implemented by an organization to protect organizational vulnerabilities from being exploited by threats
Procedures	The detailed sequential steps that are documented and inform the healthcare organization's employees on how to perform specific actions
Standards	Are consistent sets of detailed specifications followed throughout the entire healthcare organization and typically address a system or technical configuration

Practice Exam

1. ARRA is an acronym for:
   a. American Recovery and Reinvestment Act
   b. Availability, Resilience, and Readiness Act
   c. Applicable Regulations and Requirements Act
   d. American Accessibility and Readiness Act
2. HITECH Act is an acronym for:
   a. Health Information Technology for Equality and Child Health Act
   b. Health Information Technology for Economic and Clinical Health Act
   c. Health Information Transfer for Emergency and Clinical Health Act
   d. Health Information Technology for Education and Clinical Health Act
3. When U.S. healthcare organizations conduct business internationally, they do not need to be concerned with:
   a. HITECH Act
   b. UK Data Protection Act
   c. PIPEDA
   d. Safe Harbor

4. Safe Harbor is based on:
   a. HITECH Act and HIPAA
   b. Seven privacy principles
   c. EU Directive 95/46/EC
   d. Both b and c
5. DURSA is an acronym for:
   a. Data Use and Reciprocal Support Agreement
   b. Data Use and Regulatory Systems Act
   c. Data Use and Reciprocal Support Act
   d. Data Use and Regulatory Systems Agreement
6. Which of the following is not a principle of Safe Harbor?
   a. Access
   b. Enforcement
   c. Encryption
   d. Onward transfer
7. Additional regulatory requirements healthcare organizations are likely to face include:
   a. OSH Act
   b. PCI–DSS
   c. GLBA
   d. Both a and b
8. A policy:
   a. Does not apply to covered entities
   b. Details the sequential steps for healthcare employees to follow
   c. Is synonymous with a procedure
   d. Is a high-level formal document approved by senior management
9. A procedure:
   a. Is a suggestion intended to streamline a healthcare process
   b. Details the sequential steps for healthcare employees to follow
   c. Is synonymous with a guideline
   d. Is a high-level formal document approved by senior management
10. ISO:
    a. Is the International Standards Organization
    b. Offers over 30 standards related to information security best practices
    c. Provides U.S.-approved healthcare security best practices
    d. Both a and b
11. NIST:
    a. Can only be used by the U.S. government
    b. Does not apply to covered entities
    c. Can only be used for Safe Harbor compliance
    d. None of the above
12. NISTIR 7497:
    a. Must be followed according to DURSA
    b. Provides required HIPAA security controls for covered entities

    c. Is the guide for implementing the HIPAA Security Rule

    d. Is *Security Architecture Design Process for Health Information Exchanges*

13. Common Criteria:

    a. Certifies IT products

    b. Is a widely accepted framework

    c. Is managed under the CCRA

    d. All of the above

14. The IG Toolkit:

    a. Is an online self-assessment tool

    b. Allows organizations in the United Kingdom to comply with DHIG policies and standards

    c. Can be used by all types and sizes of organizations

    d. All of the above

15. The IG Toolkit assesses organizations against the following governance requirements:

    a. Management structures and responsibilities

    b. Confidentiality and data protection

    c. Information security

    d. All of the above

16. GAAP is the acronym for:

    a. Globally Accepted Privacy Principles

    b. Generally Accepted Privacy Principles

    c. Globally Accepted Privacy Practices

    d. Generally Accepted Privacy Practices

17. HITRUST:

    a. Is only recognized in the United Kingdom

    b. Cannot be used with other security frameworks

    c. Is required under HITECH Act

    d. None of the above

18. SANS 20 Critical Security Controls:

    a. Can be used by any organization

    b. Supersede NIST SP 800-53 Controls when complying with the HITECH Act

    c. Provide the most value with the fewest number of control implementations

    d. Both a and b

    e. Both a and c

19. Compensating controls:

    a. Should not be used by covered entities

    b. Should be implemented as part of a comprehensive control framework

    c. Are required under HIPAA but not the HITECH Act

    d. None of the above

20. The (ISC)^2 Code of Ethics:

    a. Applies to all members and certificate holders

    b. Holds individuals to the highest level of professional standards

    c. Has a preamble and four canons

    d. All of the above

Practice Exam Answers

1. a
2. b
3. a
4. d
5. a
6. c
7. d
8. d
9. b
10. d
11. d
12. d
13. d
14. d
15. d
16. b
17. d
18. e
19. b
20. d

References

http://www.hhs.gov/ocr/privacy/.

http://www.hhs.gov/ocr/privacy/hipaa/administrative/enforcementrule/hitechenforcementifr.html.

http://www.hhs.gov/ocr/privacy/hipaa/administrative/breachnotificationrule/.

http://ico.org.uk/for_organisations/guidance_index/~/media/documents/library/Data_Protection/Detailed_specialist_guides/data-controllers-and-data-processors-dp-guidance.pdf.

https://www.priv.gc.ca/leg_c/leg_c_p_e.asp.

http://health.state.tn.us/hipaa/.

http://eurlex.europa.eu/LexUriServ/LexUriServ.do?uri=OJ:L:2009:337:0011:0036:en:PDF.

http://ec.europa.eu/justice/data-protection/index_en.htm.

http://www.legislation.gov.uk/ukpga/1998/29/contents.

http://www.hhs.gov/ocr/privacy/hipaa/administrative/breachnotificationrule/.

http://www.hhs.gov/ocr/privacy/hipaa/administrative/enforcementrule/enfifr.pdf.

http://www.healthit.gov/sites/default/files/dursa-2009-version-for-production-pilots-20091118-1.pdf.

http://www.healthit.gov/sites/default/files/pdf/privacy/privacy-and-security-guide.pdf.

http://www.export.gov/safeharbor/eu/eg_main_018365.asp.

https://www.osha.gov/.

https://www.pcisecuritystandards.org.

http://www.sec.gov/about/laws.shtml#sox2002.

http://www.sec.gov/about/laws/soa2002.pdf.

http://www.sans.org/security-resources/policies/Policy_Primer.pdf.

http://www.iso.org/iso/home.htm.

http://nist.gov/.

http://csrc.nist.gov/publications/nistpubs/800-66-Rev1/SP-800-66-Revision1.pdf.

http://www.hpa.org.uk/web/HPAweb&HPAwebStandard/HPAweb_C/1195733746440.

http://csrc.nist.gov/publications/nistir/ir7497/nistir-7497.pdf.

https://www.commoncriteriaportal.org/.

https://www.igt.hscic.gov.uk/.

http://hitrustalliance.net/.

http://www.sans.edu/research/security-laboratory/article/security-controls.

https://www.isc2.org/ethics/default.aspx.

CHAPTER 4

Privacy and Security in Healthcare

THIS CHAPTER WILL HELP CANDIDATES:

- Understand security and privacy concepts
- Understand the relationship between security and privacy
- Understand general privacy principles and standards
- Understand sensitive data and handling implications

INTRODUCTION

Security Fundamentals

Confidentiality, integrity, and availability (CIA) are the foundational elements required to ensure privacy and security that users of the healthcare system deserve and expect. It is best to think of CIA as interrelated pillars that support privacy and security initiatives in healthcare. If any of the foundational elements are missing or vulnerable, privacy and security objectives within the healthcare system cannot be achieved. Confidentiality, integrity, and availability are often referred to as the CIA triad and usually represented in the model shown in Figure 4.1.

Confidentiality

Under HIPAA, "Confidentiality means the property that data or information is not made available or disclosed to unauthorized persons or processes." Simply put, confidentiality is about preventing unauthorized disclosure of healthcare information. Anytime sensitive healthcare information is accessed, viewed, or transmitted in an unauthorized manner, patient confidentiality is at risk.

Integrity

Integrity is formally defined by HIPAA as "Means the property that data or information have not been altered or destroyed in an unauthorized manner." It is best to think of integrity as the reliability of information. Imagine the

61

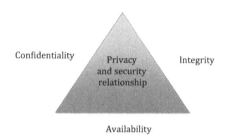

FIGURE 4.1 CIA triad.

consequences to patient healthcare delivery if medical professionals make patient care choices based on inaccurate or unreliable data.

Availability

Availability is the third essential element to the CIA triad. Healthcare professionals require patient information systems to be there when needed. When critical healthcare systems are unavailable, quality healthcare services cannot be delivered in an efficient manner. Beyond efficiency, patient care decisions are significantly impacted when system or the information contained in those systems is unavailable. In many healthcare settings the system being down can be life-threatening rather than an inconvenience. Although HIPAA formally defines availability as "The property that data or information is accessible and useable upon demand by an authorized person," one can see the importance of healthcare technology availability through the perspective of having the right tools to do the job. Modern healthcare has become reliant on technology as a tool for quality service delivery. Resilient healthcare systems are required to provide healthcare practitioners with the tools they need to perform their jobs on a daily basis. Just as in the past it would be unacceptable for a physician to visit a patient without his black bag and stethoscope, we cannot expect practitioners to provide services without high availability health information systems.

SECURITY PRINCIPLES

One of the most effective ways to ensure CIA is to take a defense-in-depth or layered approach when addressing privacy and security issues. A tiered approach avoids a single point of failure and supports layered controls in case one of the controls is compromised or does not operate as intended.

Access Control

Access control is often the first and possibly most robust controls that can be implemented to ensure privacy and security in the healthcare environment.

When you think about a typical healthcare environment and all the sensitive information present, you quickly understand the importance of limiting the access to that information to only authorized individuals who need to have access to the information in order to perform their job responsibilities and deliver healthcare services. Although similar in nature, it is important to distinguish between physical and logical access control. Since physical security is often the first line of defense we will start there. Since systems that store sensitive healthcare information are located within the physical walls of healthcare service providers, we can focus on the outside and work our way in. Considering the defense-in-depth security methodology, we are able to achieve our first layer of access control just by limiting physical access to information systems. This does not mean we do not need logical security, but rather we can gain some comfort in knowing that well-designed and properly maintained physical security access controls can deter or prevent unauthorized individuals from being able to physically access sensitive information or healthcare systems. Since we must avoid creating single points of failure and there are some threats that exist regardless of physical security controls, logical access controls are the next layer in effective security and required to support the CIA triad. Logical access controls should be developed to support the system architecture and be implemented at as many layers as possible. This typically means ensuring proper access control at both the network and system level. For example, a healthcare practitioner's access should be controlled when he or she logs into the network and again when he or she wants to access a particular system hosted on the network. From a more practical and healthcare-focused view, organizations do not want just anyone to be able to view or access patient information. So do organizations just need to implement controls preventing only outsiders from accessing patient records? The answer is no. Just because a person is employed by a healthcare organization does not mean they should be allowed to access sensitive patient information. In fact, effective access control is based on the concept of least privilege (individuals should only be able to access the information required to perform their job – no more, no less) and we will discuss in greater detail a little later. Once a healthcare organization ultimately determines who should be able to access information, the next challenge becomes the "how." Thinking back to our discussion on defense-in-depth, it makes sense that there is no single approach or access control to accomplish the task. In fact, the more layered the controls, the better. In order to understand how to best implement access controls, let us take a look at the three types of controls: administrative, physical, and technical.

It is best to think of these as independent but interconnected elements that work together to ensure appropriate levels of access control for healthcare organizations. Figure 4.2 shows the relationship among the control types.

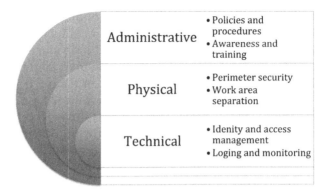

Administrative	• Policies and procedures • Awareness and training
Physical	• Perimeter security • Work area separation
Technical	• Idenity and access management • Loging and monitoring

FIGURE 4.2 Relationship of control types.

Although the three categories work together and can be implemented independently, we recommend the sequence of administrative, physical, and technical and that is the order they will be discussed in this book. Administrative controls, when supported by senior leadership, set the foundation (aka "tone at the top") for the organization's access control objectives. These are often "soft" controls based on policies and organizational culture and regulatory requirements. Physical controls are usually the first layer of defense and often provide perimeter support for technical controls. These can range from door locks and ID badge systems to physical partitions separating employee work and patient care areas. Technical controls usually reside at the system level and are the mechanisms in place to support the organization's privacy and security policies. A common example would be requiring a valid username and password before accessing the system.

Now that we have drawn the distinction between physical and logical access controls, we will review three common logical access control models. The three models commonly used in logical access control include discretionary access control (DAC), mandatory access control (MAC), and role-based access control (RBAC).

- **DAC** – Is a control mechanism where the user explicitly allows access to other users or programs that the user has ownership or control over.
- **MAC** – Is a control mechanism where the user permissions are explicitly controlled by the information system. The permissions are enforced by a collection of prebuilt access rules within the system. When the user is assigned permissions to a system object, the system restricts the activity of the user in accordance with the object's permission level. For example, a user cannot share information with unauthorized users or system objects.

- **RBAC** – Is a control mechanism based on business-specific functions within an organization. For example, the role of "Accountant" can view accounts payable information, but the role of "Accounting Manager" can perform accounts payable transactions.

Data Encryption

Encryption is a foundational component of healthcare security and privacy. It enables organization to achieve privacy and security objectives. Per the HIPAA Security Rule, protected health information (PHI) must be encrypted and encryption is defined as "the use of an algorithmic process to transform data into a form in which there is a low probability of assigning meaning without use of a confidential process or key." It is important to note that not all encryption algorithms function in the same manner and that some models and algorithms are suitable to meet specific healthcare requirements.

Although predominantly used for the protection of data, cryptography can be used for authentication. The three types of encryption algorithms include secret key (symmetric), public key (asymmetric), and hash functions.

- **Secret or symmetric key cryptography** – Utilizes one key for both encryption and decryption
- **Public or asymmetric key cryptography** – Utilizes one key for encryption and a different key for decryption
- **Hash functions** – Are used to support integrity by converting a message into a one-way irreversible hash function

Before detailing cryptography types mentioned earlier, one must understand some foundational definitions to truly appreciate how each cryptography model functions. Ciphertext is the encrypted output from an encryption algorithm. The original unencrypted data is called plaintext. Any number of encryption algorithms can be selected by the organization to convert the plaintext into ciphertext. When the ciphertext is decrypted, the data is transformed into its original readable state, the plaintext.

Secret Key Encryption

In secret key encryption, since the same key is used to encrypt and decrypt, proper safeguarding and distribution of that key is of paramount importance. If the key is shared with unauthorized or unintended recipients at any time during the information's life cycle, the protection of the information must be considered compromised. A compromised data protection, or encryption process that is considered to be compromised, cannot be relied on to support the confidentiality and integrity (the C and I elements of the CIA triangle) of the data being encrypted.

Public Key Encryption

Public key encryption uses two different keys. One key is used to encrypt the information and the other is used to decrypt the information. Sometimes this is referred to as asymmetric encryption because two keys are required to make the system and/or process work securely. One key is known as the public key and should be shared by the owner with anyone who will be securely communicating with the key owner. However, the owner's secret key is not to be shared and considered a private key. If the private key is shared with unauthorized recipients, the encryption mechanisms protecting the information must be considered compromised.

Hash Functions

It is important to know that the slight technical differences that support hashing are significant enough to draw a distinction between symmetric or asymmetric cryptography and hash functions. Hashing only supports integrity and not confidentiality services. A hash function is a one-way cryptographic algorithm. The use of a one-way cryptographic algorithm means that the ciphertext cannot be decrypted to reveal the original plaintext. The algorithm is made of two parts. The first element is the original content and is called the message. After encryption, the output, or second element, is called the message digest. The message digest is a unique identifier and based on the message. It is often viewed as a digital fingerprint. If the original message were altered in anyway, then it would not match the original message digest. Table 4.1 compares the types of encryption algorithms as well as provides a common example.

Table 4.1 Common Encryption Algorithms

Encryption Type	Strengths	Weakness	Example
Symmetric	• Faster than asymmetric systems • Difficult to break when large key size is used	• Requires secure mechanism to deliver keys • Key management is difficult due to high volume of keys • Cannot perform non-repudiation	• AES • 3DES
Asymmetric	• Stronger key distribution • Improved scalability • Provides integrity, authenticity, and non-repudiation functions	• Slower than symmetric systems • Mathematically intense work factor	• RSA • DSA
Hash function	• One-way efficiency • Provides file/message integrity	• Does not support confidentiality	• SHA 1 • MD5

Training and Awareness

Although training and awareness should be a cornerstone of an organization's healthcare security program, they are often an underutilized security strategy. When managed properly, it can be a powerful tool for educating and reminding the organization's workforce on security, privacy, and regulatory requirements. Training is a specific curriculum intended to teach individuals the specific skills needed to perform their job responsibilities.

Awareness is a more general program with a broader audience (i.e., the entire organization) intended to educate and remind employees about adhering to security and privacy initiatives to support the organization's healthcare security, privacy, and regulatory requirements. Training and awareness are people-focused activities and therefore need to be managed differently than a specific security or privacy technology. Unlike an automated system process or configuration setting, people have (and often do have) the ability to stray from organization best practices. One of the most effective ways to overcome this challenge is to design, implement, and manage effective training and awareness programs. Our emphasis will be on security awareness and privacy programs (as these are more universal in nature and applicable to all healthcare organizations) but assume that organizations will deploy specific training programs (suited to their specific technologies and processes) under the following best practices:

- Training tailored to organizational-specific technologies (e.g., CCNA® certified engineers if your organization uses Cisco networking and firewall equipment)
- Regulatory specific training for compliance personnel (e.g., HIPAA, Records Management, Safe Harbor)

NIST Special Publication 800-16 details specific recommendations for successful training and awareness programs but the following elements should be included:

- Clearly defined learning objectives
- Relevant and "user-friendly" content and delivery
- Metrics and measurements (for program delivery and continuous improvement)
- Student evaluation and performance tracking
- Implementation and tracking evidence (for regulatory compliance and audit purposes)

When healthcare organizations design, build, deploy, and manage robust training and awareness programs, they are receiving several benefits. Figure 4.3 depicts the cultural benefits of organizations adopting a strong training and awareness program. Not only are they adhering to best practices and complying

FIGURE 4.3 Training and awareness relationship.

with specific healthcare security and privacy requirements, but also additionally they are creating a security-aware and proactive security- and privacy-focused culture for their organization.

Logging and Monitoring

Once an organization implements controls to safeguard healthcare information, it is essential they log and monitor the activities associated with said controls. An audit log is a system-generated chronology of events and activity associated with that system. Audit logs are typically highly configurable but most organizations focus on logging access and operational activity associated with the system. Monitoring works in conjunction with logging and is the systematic process of reviewing activity based on specific thresholds defined in the audit log configuration. HIPAA requires the following three activities associated with logging and monitoring:

Term	Description	HIPAA Reference
Log-in monitoring	Monitoring system log-in and access for discrepancies. The requirement applies to "log-in attempts" including both failed and successful log-ins	164.308(a)(5)(ii)(C)
Audit controls	Cover audit logging and other audit trails on systems that deal with sensitive health information	164.312(b)
Information system activity review	Regularly reviews records of information system activity such as audit logs, access reports, and security incident tracking	164.308(a)(1)(ii)(D)

Vulnerability Management

NIST Special Publication 800-53 Rev. 4 defines vulnerability management as "The systematic examination of an information system or product to determine the adequacy of security measures, identify security deficiencies, provide data

Vulnerability   Vulnerability
identification   remediation

FIGURE 4.4 Vulnerability management cycle.

from which to predict the effectiveness of proposed security measures, and confirm the adequacy of such measures after implementation." As demonstrated in Figure 4.4, when performed correctly, vulnerability management is a continuous process that includes the identification and remediation of vulnerabilities.

As part of a more comprehensive security management process HIPAA requires a systematic vulnerability management program that includes the following elements: program evaluation, security management process, risk analysis, risk management, information system activity review, incident procedures, and awareness and training.

Requirement	Description	HIPAA Reference
Program evaluation	"Perform a periodic technical and nontechnical evaluation based initially upon the standards implemented under this rule and subsequently, in response to environmental or operational changes affecting the security of electronic protected health information, that establishes the extent to which an entity's security policies and procedures meet the requirements of this subpart."	(a)(8)
Risk analysis and management	• "Conduct an accurate and thorough assessment of the potential risks and vulnerabilities to the confidentiality, integrity, and availability of electronic protected health information held by the covered entity." And • "Implement security measures sufficient to reduce risks and vulnerabilities to a reasonable and appropriate level ..."	(a)(1)(ii)(A) and (a)(1)(ii)(B)

System activity review	"Implement procedures to regularly review records of information system activity, such as audit logs, access reports, and security incident tracking reports."	(a)(1)(ii)(D)
Incident procedures	"Implement policies and procedures to address security incidents."	(a)(6)(i) and (a)(6)(ii)
Awareness and training	"Implement a security awareness and training program for all members of its workforce (including management)."	(a)(5)(i)

Figure 4.5 shows how the five specific elements support a comprehensive vulnerability program required by HIPAA.

Systems Recovery

Systems recovery and contingency planning is the series of processes and procedures that healthcare organizations implement to ensure availability (remember the availability leg of the CIA triangle) of electronic protected health information (EPHI). All healthcare organizations should develop a comprehensive business resiliency program to ensure the availability of healthcare information against natural or man-made disruptions. In addition to contingency planning being a security best practice, the HIPAA Contingency Plan Standard also addresses the importance of contingency planning through five implementation specifications. Per the HIPAA Standard [§164.308(a)(7)(ii)(A)–(E)] the five contingency plan implementation standards are a data backup plan (required), disaster recovery plan (required), emergency mode operation plan (required), testing and revision procedures

FIGURE 4.5 HIPAA vulnerability program elements.

(addressable), and application and data criticality analysis (addressable) and are defined as follows:

- **Data backup plan**: "Establish and implement procedures to create and maintain retrievable exact copies of electronic protected health information."
- **Disaster recovery plan**: "Establish (and implement as needed) procedures to restore any loss of data."
- **Emergency mode operation plan**: "Establish (and implement as needed) procedures to enable continuation of critical business processes for protection of the security of electronic protected health information while operating in emergency mode."
- **Testing and revision procedures**: "Implement procedures for periodic testing and revision of contingency plans."
- **Application and data criticality analysis**: "Assess the relative criticality of specific applications and data in support of other contingency plan components."

Segregation of Duties

Segregation of duties mandates that sensitive job functions that, when combined, have a high potential for abuse should be performed by separate people in order to reduce that risk of abuse. This is often accomplished by having at least two individuals (one to perform and one to approve) involved to ensure a system of checks and balances. For example, if a server configuration change needs to be made to support a software installation for a developer, the developer cannot directly make that change. He or she would request the change be made, and after approval from management, a system administrator would make the changes for the developer.

Least Privilege

According to NIST Special Publication 800-12 least privilege is defined as "the security objective of granting users only those accesses they need to perform their official duties." From a HIPAA perspective, the Privacy Rule typically requires covered entities to take reasonable actions to limit the disclosure of PHI to the least amount required to accomplish the intended task. In addition to providing users the least amount of access needed to perform their jobs, healthcare organizations also need to routinely review that privileges are still needed and appropriate for the user's current role. In a busy healthcare organization, it is common for an employee's job function to change and they may no longer need the same level of permissions for their new role within the organization.

Business Continuity and Disaster Recovery

Business continuity is a relatively broad concept and often means different things to different organizations. However, in its simplest form, business continuity is about ensuring an organization's critical business functions are available and continue to operate during an incident or emergency. Each organization will need to define what critical operations are, as well as what an incident or emergency is, and business continuity and disaster recovery planning accomplish this. Business continuity planning is the process that organizations follow so they can implement policies, procedures, processes, and technology used to ensure how an organization's business objectives will be performed after a significant disruption. It is important to note that a variety (both natural and man-made) of events (e.g., flood, terrorism) can define a significant disruption and organizations must plan accordingly. Additionally, patients have high expectations that healthcare organizations have the ability to provide critical services and patient care regardless of a significant disruption. In fact, if the event is regional or national in nature (e.g., an entire state is impacted by a pandemic), there may be an even greater expectation or need that healthcare organizations can deliver patient care services. Disaster recovery planning is similar in nature to business continuity planning and they often work in conjunction to support the healthcare organization's short- and long-term needs when recovering from a significant and disruptive unplanned event. A useful perspective on the relationship is that business continuity is about building systems and processes that are resilient to disruptions and disaster recovery is about systems and processes that enable the organization to quickly recover from a disruption. Disaster recovery tends to focus on the short-term response after a disaster occurs. Typically it focuses on the organization's critical systems (essential to providing healthcare services) in a timely manner (e.g., the pharmacy system needs to be available within 2 h of a disaster). Although each healthcare organization will determine its specific needs, and several factors should go into a disaster recovery planning, the following elements are essential to a comprehensive disaster recovery plan:

- **Critical application assessment** – Determining which systems are essential to the healthcare organization delivering critical services.
- **Backup procedures** – Determining the details (e.g., who, what, when) and steps for backing up systems and data.
- **Recovery procedures** – Determining the details (e.g., who, what, when) and steps for recovering data and systems from backup after a disaster.
- **Implementation procedures** – Determining how to best implement the selected procedures.
- **Test procedures** – Developing test procedures so that testing can be performed on a regular basis to ensure the organization is capable of recovering after a disaster.

Before an appropriate backup strategy can be selected, it is important to understand the fundamentals of backups. Essentially, backups can be managed as onsite or remote. However, most healthcare organizations will determine that a hybrid approach offers the best solution since there are both advantages and disadvantages to each strategy.

- **Onsite backups** – Allow organizations to store the data onsite, the advantage being they are readily available if needed. One disadvantage is that if the onsite location is unavailable or destroyed, so are the backup data. Another disadvantage is that the physical backup media (and information it contains) must be properly safeguarded.
- **Remote backups** – Allow organizations to store the data offsite, the advantage being that if the location is unavailable or destroyed, the backup data still exist. The disadvantage is that it can be time consuming or difficult to obtain backup data in a timely manner when they are not located onsite.

Another important factor when discussing backups is the frequency and specific methodology. Each method has advantages and disadvantages and most healthcare organizations select a hybrid approach to best meet their specific needs. The most common types include the following:

- **Full backup** – Includes all data and is slower to backup but faster to restore and requires the most storage space.
- **Incremental backup** – Only includes new or modified data, is fast to backup, has a moderate restore time, and requires lower storage space.
- **Differential backup** – Includes all changed data since the last full backup, has a moderate time frame to backup, and requires moderate storage space.
- **Mirrored backup** – Only includes new or modified data and has the fastest backup and restore times, but requires the most storage space.

Healthcare organizations should develop a compressive program and supporting documentation to support their backup strategy. This is used to clarify expectations and execution details. It is best to answer the "five W's plus one" (who, what, when, where, why, and how) questions when documenting the backup strategy. Since both improvements to backup technology and the substantial reduction in cost for backup technology have occurred in recent years, healthcare organizations have additional alternatives (rather than traditional tape or other storage media) to consider when developing their backup strategies. This includes alternative sites, high availability architectures and technologies, and real-time journaling. Additionally, the capabilities associated with alternate sites need to also be considered by the healthcare organization's strategy. The three most common considerations include a hot site, cold site, and warm site.

- **Hot sites** – Duplicate the primary production site in terms of both infrastructure and data. The main advantage is that there is little to no time required to shift operations from the original production site to the alternative site. The primary disadvantage is the costs and maintenance associated with fully duplicating a production environment.

- **Cold sites** – Have the primary advantage of being low cost, since the information system hardware and backup data are not present at the cold site. The disadvantage is the time and effort required to establish a production-level environment.
- **Warm sites** – Are a hybrid alternative to hot and cold sites. The advantage is that they cost less than a hot site, but have more robust capabilities than a cold site.

Data Retention and Destruction

Data retention and destruction policies and procedures involve the healthcare organization's specifications for retaining and destroying data in accordance with legal, regulatory, and business requirements. The HIPAA Privacy Rule requires that covered entities apply appropriate administrative, technical, and physical safeguards to protect the privacy of PHI, in any form. This applies to the disposal of such information when the data are no longer required or a specific data retention period has expired. Additionally, the HIPAA Security Rule requires that covered entities implement policies and procedures to address the final disposition of EPHI and/or the hardware or electronic media on which it is stored, as well as to implement procedures for removal of EPHI from electronic media before the media are made available for reuse.

Since both the HIPAA Privacy and Security Rules address data retention and destruction, healthcare organizations must implement the appropriate safeguards to protect PHI and comply with HIPAA requirements.

GENERAL PRIVACY PRINCIPLES

There are 12 general privacy principles we will be discussing that are applicable to the 4 commonly recognized healthcare privacy standards. The four healthcare privacy standards are:

- Organization for Economic Co-operation and Development (OECD) Privacy Principles
- Generally Accepted Privacy Principles (GAPP)
- Personal Information Protection and Electronic Documents Act (PIPEDA)
- UK Data Protection Act 1998 (DPA)

We will be detailing the 4 healthcare privacy standards later in the chapter, but understanding the 12 general privacy principles provides a solid foundation and the 4 healthcare privacy standards are based on the privacy principles.

Although there are slight differences between how each standard utilizes the 12 principles, the intent and overall commonality of each principle is applicable.

12 Privacy Principles

The 12 principles and their descriptions are listed as follows:

- **Consent/Choice** – Permission granted from the patient or their legal guardian to an organization to use protected health information (PHI) for lawful healthcare purposes (treatment, research, operations, etc.).
- **Limited Collection/Legitimate Purpose/Purpose Specification** – The principle that states that the purposes for which personal data are collected should be specified not later than at the time of data collection and the subsequent use limited to the fulfillment of those purposes or such others as are not incompatible with those purposes and as are specified on each occasion of change of purpose.
- **Disclosure Limitation/Transfer to Third Parties/Trans-Border Concerns** – Specifies that personal information can only be disclosed for the purposes identified under notice and consent. It may also mean that personal data be disclosed outside of jurisdictional boundaries.
- **Access Limitation** – This usually ensures that access to information is limited only to individuals who specifically require access. Under the DPA, it means appropriate safeguards to prevent unauthorized access to personal data.
- **Security** – Organizations must have safeguards to protect personal information.
- **Accuracy, Completeness, Quality** – This principle specifies that organizations in possession of personal information are responsible for ensuring its accuracy, completeness, and quality.
- **Management, Designation of Privacy Officer, Supervisor Re-Authority, Processing Authorization, Accountability** – These principles ensure that the organization has formally assigned accountability to safeguarding personal information under its control.
- **Transparency, Openness** – Organizations must make their policies readily available to individuals and be clear on the intended use of an individual's personal information.
- **Proportionality, Use and Retention, Use Limitation** – This principle protects an individual's healthcare information by restricting the use of data and ensuring that organizations destroy information when it is no longer in use.
- **Access, Individual Participation** –This principle states that individuals have the right to request from organizations a verification of whether or not the organization has information about them.

- **Notice, Purpose Specification** – Is a principle that ensures that organizations provide notice to individuals about the organizations' policies and procedures regarding the collection, retention, and disclosure of data.
- **Additional Measures for Breach Notification** – Is a principle to ensure that organizations have specific policies and procedures for notifying individuals in the event of a data breach.

Now that we have a detailed understanding of the 12 general privacy principles we can see how they relate to the 4 specific healthcare standards listed in the following. It is important to note that since 4 different authorities issued the standards, there may be some slight differences, and in some cases not all of the 12 general privacy principles may directly apply. However, since the principles are rooted in the fundamentals of privacy, it is best to focus on the spirit or intent of the standard or law rather than the letter of the standard or law.

Data Privacy Standards
Organization for Economic Co-Operation and Development Privacy Principles

According to the OECD, their mission is to "promote policies that will improve the economic and social well-being of the world." Although the OECD achieves their mission in many ways and provides invaluable guidance in a number of areas, our focus will be on the privacy principles. In terms of exam preparation, focusing on the 12 general privacy principles, and applying foundational privacy knowledge to the mission and organizational aspects of the OECD will suffice for exam preparation. Since OECD has an international presence, and works with organizations across the world, they can leverage the 12 privacy principles to address healthcare privacy from an international perspective.

Generally Accepted Privacy Principles

The American Institute of Certified Public Accountants and the Canadian Institute of Chartered Accountants sponsor the GAPP. Their guidance is intended to provide a framework for organizations looking to implement a privacy program. In comparison to the OECD, the GAPP has a business perspective and less of an international focus and may not address all specific local, national, or international privacy laws. However, it is still grounded in the 12 general privacy principles and enables organizations insight on how to properly safeguard healthcare information and manage effective privacy programs.

Personal Information Protection and Electronic Documents Act

The PIPEDA is the framework set forth by Canada's Office of the Privacy Commissioner. It applies to both federal and private sector organizations and governs the collection, use, and disclosure of personal information. One of the most significant aspects of PIPEDA is that it enables individuals the right to access (and correct if necessary) their personal information if it was collected by federal and private entities. PIPEDA, as with GAPP and OECD, is based on the 12 general privacy principles discussed earlier.

UK Data Protection Act 1998

The UK Data Protection Act of 1998, commonly referred to as DPA, is an independent authority in the United Kingdom, responsible for allowing access to official information and protecting personal information. One of the ways this is accomplished is through the United Kingdom's Information Commissioner's Office (ICO). All organizations, unless specifically exempt, that possess and/or use personal information must register with the Commissioner's Office. The UK DPA also uses eight data protection principles to ensure personal information is properly safeguarded. The ICO specifically states the following:

1. Personal data shall be processed fairly and lawfully and, in particular, shall not be processed unless:
   a. At least one of the conditions in Schedule 2 is met, and
   b. In the case of sensitive personal data, at least one of the conditions in Schedule 3 is also met.
2. Personal data shall be obtained only for one or more specified and lawful purposes, and shall not be further processed in any manner incompatible with that purpose or those purposes.
3. Personal data shall be adequate, relevant, and not excessive in relation to the purpose or purposes for which they are processed.
4. Personal data shall be accurate and, where necessary, kept up to date.
5. Personal data processed for any purpose or purposes shall not be kept for longer than is necessary for that purpose or those purposes.
6. Personal data shall be processed in accordance with the rights of data subjects under this Act.
7. Appropriate technical and organizational measures shall be taken against unauthorized or unlawful processing of personal data and against accidental loss or destruction of, or damage to, personal data.
8. Personal data shall not be transferred to a country or territory outside the European Economic Area unless that country or territory ensures an adequate level of protection for the rights and freedoms of data subjects in relation to the processing of personal data.

Another important element of the DPA to take notice of is the restrictions it holds for data transfer and use outside of the European Economic Area. Otherwise, like the other 3 privacy standards, the DPA is based on the 12 privacy principles.

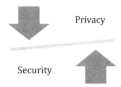

FIGURE 4.6 Privacy and security relationship.

RELATIONSHIP BETWEEN PRIVACY AND SECURITY

Although there can be some inherent conflicts between privacy and security, security is required to support privacy objectives. Therefore, there is a very close relationship and it is understood that some privacy issues (e.g., monitoring and data collection) are caused when implementing sound security practices. Most organizations will find they need to balance elements of the privacy and security relationship to properly safeguard PHI. Figure 4.6 depicts the privacy and security relationship.

Some of the more common privacy issues impacting security include network and system monitoring, background investigations, supplier and partner relationships, and information sharing programs. Organizational privacy objectives and requirements are accomplished by the implementation of security controls. Looking back the CIA triangle, privacy is supported by the confidentiality and integrity legs of the triangle.

THE DISPARATE NATURE OF SENSITIVE DATA AND HANDLING IMPLICATIONS

Healthcare organizations are responsible for the implementation of safeguards in order to protect sensitive patient data. Healthcare organizations and the information systems they rely on have massive amounts of data. Before the organization can select the appropriate controls and safeguards they must understand what they are trying to protect and why. Although more detailed strategies are discussed in the risk management sections of this text, data classification is one of the first steps. If you do not structure and organize the data, how can you prioritize and protect it? Furthermore, not all data and information are equal in value, so all data sets do not need to be managed, protected, and handled the same way.

Data classification schemas allow healthcare organizations to classify and label their data. These organizational-based standards and definitions allow for effective communication and understanding and enable employees to have a uniform understanding of the data and associated precautions within their organization. Although there may be slight variances and specific organizational differences in data classification models, they are based on the common principles. These typically include a hierarchical structure and clearly defined labels and definitions to ensure information is handled consistently.

Once the data are properly classified, organizations need to create detailed handling procedures that address the following data handling elements:

- **Access** – Who can access the data?
- **Use** – Why is it needed? Principle of least privilege.
- **Destruction** – How is the information destroyed after acceptable use?

Disparate data are commonly defined as data that are dissimilar in nature. This usually means differences in type, quality, format, and source. Considering the overall complexity (large number of separate and distinct organizations and systems with extensive data sharing and interdependencies) of the healthcare delivery system disparate data can be a complex challenge.

Specifically, this operating model causes the following data problems:

- **Continuation and formation of data silos** – e.g., each healthcare organization (or distinct unit within an organization) will create a separate patient record
- **Data duplication and regeneration** – e.g., separate systems (billing and pharmacy systems) containing duplicate information for the same patient
- **Lack of standardized data formats** – e.g., variance in patient record formats

In addition to making intersystem and organizational data sharing difficult, disparate data create an increased security risk. The more instances of confidential patient information, the greater the risk exposure becomes. Electronic medical records (EMRs) are intended to consolidate disparate data from all of the independent systems (e.g., pharmacy, billing, insurance) within a healthcare organization. Although this reduces many of the security concerns with disparate data referenced earlier, additional privacy and security challenges still remain. Specifically, a majority of the data types within an EMR need to be safeguarded and comply with the HIPAA Privacy Rule.

Protected Health Information

PHI is defined as any information in the medical record or designated record set that can be used to identify an individual and that was created, used, or disclosed in the course of providing a healthcare service such as diagnosis or treatment under HIPAA. The HIPAA Privacy Rule protects the 18 common identifiers listed as follows that are often associated with medical records:

1. Names
2. All geographic subdivisions smaller than a State, including street address, city, county, precinct, zip code, and their equivalent geocodes, except for the initial three digits of a zip code, if according to the current publicly available data from the Bureau of the Census: (a) the geographic unit formed by combining all zip codes with the same three initial digits contains more than 20,000 people; and (b) the initial three digits of a zip code for all such geographic units containing 20,000 or fewer people is changed to 000
3. All elements of dates (except year) for dates directly related to an individual, including birth date, admission date, discharge date, date of death; and all ages over 89 and all elements of dates (including year) indicative of such age, except that such ages and elements may be aggregated into a single category of age 90 or older
4. Phone numbers
5. Fax numbers
6. Electronic mail addresses
7. Social Security numbers
8. Medical record numbers
9. Health plan beneficiary numbers
10. Account numbers
11. Certificate/license numbers
12. Vehicle identifiers and serial numbers, including license plate numbers
13. Device identifiers and serial numbers
14. Web Universal Resource Locators (URLs)
15. Internet Protocol (IP) address numbers
16. Biometric identifiers, including fingerprints and voiceprints
17. Full face photographic images and any comparable images
18. Any other unique identifying number, characteristic, or code (note this does not mean the unique code assigned by the investigator to code the data)

The HIPAA Privacy Rule prescribes 18 identifiers that usually need to be properly safeguarded under HIPAA requirements. However, when separated (as opposed to multiple single patient identifiers in aggregate), data identifiers may not necessarily be designated as PHI. For example, a patient's name in isolation would not be considered PHI since the name alone is not directly connected with that individual's other PHI and the name would be considered publicly available information. Healthcare organizations need to be very cautious since data sets and the 18 protected identifiers can quickly change context, thus requiring organizations to comply with HIPAA Privacy and Security Safeguards. In the previous example, a name (not associated with any other identifiers) was considered public information and not considered to be PHI. However, that same name associated with additional healthcare data (e.g., patient treatment and billing information) would be considered PHI and would be required to be protected in accordance with the HIPAA Privacy and Security Rules. Now that we understand the relationship between data sets, PHI, and the 18 protected identifiers, we need to discuss some specific mitigation strategies to ensure HIPAA compliance. These fall under the category of data de-identification.

Data De-Identification

The HIPAA Privacy Rule contains a de-identification standard. The standard prescribes that health information is not individually identifiable if (1) it does not identify an individual and (2) the covered entity has no reasonable basis to believe it can be used to identify an individual. The HIPAA Privacy Rule continues to support this standard in sections 164.514(b) and (c) by specifying two acceptable methods for de-identification of data. These methods include Expert Determination and Safe Harbor. Expert Determination states that an organization may only determine information is not individually identifiable if:

1. A person with appropriate knowledge of and experience with generally accepted statistical and scientific principles and methods for rendering information is not individually identifiable;
2. Applying such principles and methods, it is determined that the risk is very small that the information could be used, alone or in combination with other reasonably available information, by an anticipated recipient to identify an individual who is a subject of the information; and
3. The methods and results of the analysis are documented in a way that justifies such determination.

The Safe Harbor method is the removal of certain identifiers (from the list of the 18 identifiers listed earlier) of the individual or of relatives, employers, or household members of the individual, where the covered entity does not have actual knowledge that the information could be used alone or in combination with other information to identify the individual who is the subject of the information.

Data Anonymization

Data anonymization can also be considered by covered entities that are leveraging data-driven research analysis projects (e.g., data mining, predictive analytics). However, it is important to point out the risks associated with these types of efforts. There are many tools, technologies, and methodologies that can be used to reverse engineer or de-anonymize data sets. Additionally, the manipulation and generation of new data from existing data (i.e., metadata) may require patient consent. When complying with the HIPAA Privacy Rule, it is important to note that sensitive health information falls under the Privacy Rule requirements regardless of delivery or recording formats. This means that both oral and recorded patient health information must be properly safeguarded. It is also important to note that HIPAA includes the protection of mental health data in its scope of coverage. In addition to mental health specifications, the following healthcare areas are also protected by HIPAA:

- **Substance abuse** – Substance abuse programs may not share patient information outside of the program.
- **Pregnancy** – Is not considered a preexisting condition, but all other health insurance requirements still exist.
- **HIV research data** – Originally not included under HIPAA.
- **DNA** – Not specifically protected, but considered to be PHI.

Many of the healthcare-specific services under HIPAA's coverage are quite intuitive. However, we must not forget the services that support healthcare delivery must also be compliant with HIPAA requirements. Figure 4.7 depicts the relationship that business support functions have with HIPAA compliance. At the highest level, any business data, system, or service used to support or deliver healthcare falls under HIPAA's regulatory authority.

The following is a list of the more common business elements associated with the support or delivery of healthcare:

- General administrative data
- Financial/accounting data
- Actuarial data

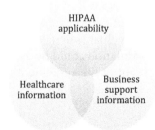

FIGURE 4.7 Business support functions' relationship with HIPAA compliance.

KEY TERMS

Access control	Is a mechanism used to restrict access to a place or resource. It can apply to both physical and logical resources and is typically composed of administrative, technical, or physical controls
Authorization	The explicit permission from the object owner that allows a subject to access a resource
Business associate	A person who on behalf of a covered entity (or of an organized healthcare arrangement in which the covered entity participates) performs or assists in the performance of:

- A function or activity involving the use or disclosure of individually identifiable health information, including claims processing or administration, data analysis, processing or administration, utilization review, quality assurance, billing, benefit management, practice management, and repricing;
- Any other function or activity regulated by this subchapter; or
- A person who provides legal, actuarial, accounting, consulting, data aggregation, management, administrative, accreditation, or financial services to or for such covered entity (or to or for an organized healthcare arrangement in which the covered entity participates) where the provision of the service involves the disclosure of individually identifiable health information from such covered entity (or arrangement), or from another business associate of such covered entity (or arrangement), to the person

Consent	Permission granted by the patient or the patient's guardian to use or disclose protected health information for purposes of treatment, payment, or healthcare operations
Covered entities	Under HIPAA means:

- A health plan
- A healthcare clearinghouse
- A healthcare provider who transmits any health information in electronic form in connection with a transaction covered under HIPAA requirements

De-identified information	Health information that does not identify an individual and with respect to which there is no reasonable basis to believe that the information can be used to identify an individual is not individually identifiable health information
Disclosure	Disclosure means the release, transfer, provision of, access to, or divulging in any other manner of information outside the entity holding the information
Group Health Plan	An employee welfare benefit plan, including insured and self-insured plans, to the extent that the plan provides medical care, including items and services paid for as medical care, to employees or their dependents directly or through insurance, reimbursement, or otherwise

Healthcare operations	Any of the following activities of the covered entity to the extent that the activities are related to covered functions:
	<ul><li>Conducting quality assessment and improvement activities</li><li>Reviewing the competence or qualifications of healthcare professionals</li><li>Underwriting, premium rating, and other activities relating to the creation, renewal, or replacement of a contract of health insurance or health benefits</li><li>Conducting or arranging for medical review, legal services, and auditing functions</li><li>Business planning and development</li><li>Business management and general administrative activities of the entity</li></ul>
Health information	Any information, oral or recorded in any medium, that is created or received by a healthcare provider, health plan, public health authority, employer, life insurer, school or university, or healthcare clearinghouse; and relates to the past, present, or future physical or mental health or condition of an individual; the provision of healthcare to an individual; or the past, present, or future payment for the provision of healthcare to an individual
Individual	The person who is the subject of protected health information
Individually identifiable health information	Information that is a subset of health information, including demographic information collected from an individual, and:
	<ul><li>Is created or received by a healthcare provider, health plan, employer, or healthcare clearinghouse; and</li><li>Relates to the past, present, or future physical or mental health or condition of an individual; the provision of healthcare to an individual; or the past, present, or future payment for the provision of healthcare to an individual; and</li><li>That identifies the individual; or</li><li>With respect to which there is a reasonable basis to believe the information can be used to identify the individual</li></ul>
Institutional review board (IRB)	An IRB is a board, committee, or other group formally designated by an institution to review research, involving humans as subjects. IRBs have authority to approve, require modification to, or disapprove all research activities covered by the HHS and FDA protection of human subjects regulations
Limited data set	A limited data set excludes specified direct identifiers of the individual or of relatives, employers, or household members of the individual
Need-to-know	A security principle that states a user should only be able to access the data they need to perform their job
Plan administration functions	An administration function performed by the Plan Sponsor of a Group Health Plan on behalf of the Group Health Plan and excludes functions performed by the Plan Sponsor in connection with any other benefit or benefit plan of the Plan Sponsor

Protected health information	Individually identifiable health information that is or has been electronically maintained or electronically transmitted by a covered entity, as well as such information when it takes any other form that (1) is created or received by a healthcare provider, health plan, employer, or healthcare clearinghouse; and (2) relates to the past, present, or future physical or mental health or condition of an individual, the provision of healthcare to an individual, or the past, present, or future payment for the provision of healthcare to an individual
Treatment	The provision, coordination, or management of healthcare and related services among healthcare providers or by a healthcare provider with a third party, consultation between healthcare providers regarding a patient, or the referral of a patient from one healthcare provider to another
Unique user identifier	A combination name/number assigned and maintained in security procedures for identifying and tracking individual user identity
Use	With respect to individually identifiable health information, the sharing, employment, application, utilization, examination, or analysis of such information with an entity that maintains such information

Practice Exam

1. Which element of CIA security model is least important?
   a. Availability – Data security is the primary concern; as long as the data are secure, availability does not matter.
   b. Confidentiality – HIPAA already ensures patient healthcare information, so we do not have to worry about confidentiality in the CIA security model.
   c. Availability – Strong access controls already ensure information is only available to authorized healthcare employees.
   d. None – All elements of the CIA security model are equally important.
2. Confidentiality is best accomplished by which of the following?
   a. Encryption
   b. Data backup systems
   c. Logical system controls that enforce data validation
   d. Vulnerability management
3. The three broad types of access control are:
   a. Confidentiality, integrity, availability
   b. Confidential, sensitive, public
   c. Administrative, physical, technical
   d. Discretionary, mandatory, role-based
4. Sensitive data should be encrypted:
   a. At rest
   b. In transit

     c. Only when leaving the organization's network

     d. Both a and b

5. Security awareness training:
   a. Only needs to be given to new employees
   b. Does not need to be given since healthcare employees receive this training when they receive their healthcare training and certification
   c. Should be given to all employees on an annual basis
   d. Only needs to be given to employees who handle PHI

6. Audit logging:
   a. Only needs to be performed 1 month prior to an audit
   b. Should be performed in conjunction with monitoring
   c. Does not need to be performed by covered entities (only healthcare organizations)
   d. Does not need to be performed by healthcare organizations (only covered entities)

7. Vulnerability management includes:
   a. Identification and remediation
   b. A continuous process
   c. Remediation only
   d. Both a and b

8. Segregation of duties:
   a. Does not apply to covered entities
   b. Is not required when encryption is being used
   c. Is designed to reduce the risk of system abuse
   d. Only applies to larger organizations since having more employees increases the risk for system abuse

9. Business continuity:
   a. Only applies to covered entities since they are businesses that support healthcare organizations rather than deliver patient healthcare services
   b. Is composed of many technologies and processes that support the availability leg of the CIA triangle
   c. Is optional for covered entities since they do not provide direct patient care
   d. None of the above

10. Data destruction includes:
    a. Shredding
    b. Degaussing
    c. None of the above
    d. Both a and b

11. OECD focuses their mission on serving:
    a. The United States
    b. People around the world
    c. The United Kingdom
    d. North America

12. GAPP applies to:
    a. Federal organizations in the United States and Canada
    b. The United States and Canada
    c. The United States only
    d. Canada only
13. PIPEDA stands for:
    a. Personal Information Protection and Electronic Documents Act
    b. Privacy Information Protection and Electronic Document Act
    c. Personal Information Protection and Electronic Data Act
    d. Privacy Information Protection and Electronic Data Act
14. The UK DPA:
    a. Involves the Information Commissioner's Office
    b. Has restrictions on data transfer outside of the European Economic Area
    c. Contains eight specific data protection principles
    d. All of the above
15. Consent/Choice is:
    a. Not important in healthcare setting since healthcare organizations need to have PHI to perform service requested by the patient
    b. Should be discussed with the patient prior to delivering any services
    c. Is only relevant for healthcare-related research, not traditional patient care services
    d. Only applies to US entities following GAAP
16. The accuracy privacy principle:
    a. Requires organizations to maintain complete and reliable PHI
    b. Is applicable to GAAP
    c. Is applicable to PIPEDA
    d. All of the above
17. Breach notification requirements:
    a. Are only important for transborder data flows
    b. Do not apply if the PHI was for testing and research purposes
    c. Both a and b
    d. None of the above
18. The relationship between privacy and security:
    a. Is symbiotic and both are relevant to safeguarding PHI
    b. Is not relevant since privacy and security are two separate and distinct disciplines
    c. Is not relevant since privacy is more important than security
    d. Is not relevant since security is more important than privacy
19. Under the HIPAA Privacy Rule, there are:
    a. 18 possible identifiers of PHI
    b. 81 possible identifiers of PHI
    c. 8 possible identifies of PHI
    d. No specific number as it depends on the organization's use of PHI

20. De-identification and anonymization are:
    a. Synonymous
    b. Two methods for preventing disclosure of PHI
    c. Both a and b
    d. None of the above

Practice Exam Answers

1. d
2. a
3. c
4. d
5. c
6. b
7. d
8. c
9. b
10. d
11. b
12. b
13. a
14. d
15. b
16. d
17. d
18. a
19. a
20. b

References

http://www.hhs.gov/ocr/privacy/hipaa/administrative/securityrule/index.html.

http://www.hhs.gov/ocr/privacy/hipaa/administrative/securityrule/securityrulepdf.pdf.

http://www.hhs.gov/ocr/privacy/hipaa/administrative/privacyrule/index.html.

http://www.hhs.gov/ocr/privacy/hipaa/administrative/privacyrule/privruletxt.txt.

http://www.oecd.org/internet/ieconomy/oecdguidelinesontheprotectionofprivacyandtransbor-derflowsofpersonaldata.htm.

http://www.aicpa.org/INTERESTAREAS/INFORMATIONTECHNOLOGY/RESOURCES/PRIVACY/GENERALLYACCEPTEDPRIVACYPRINCIPLES/Pages/default.aspx.

http://www.priv.gc.ca/leg_c/leg_c_p_e.asp.

http://www.legislation.gov.uk/ukpga/1998/29/contents.

http://csrc.nist.gov/publications/fips/fips140-2/fips1402.pdf.

http://csrc.nist.gov/publications/nistpubs/800-122/sp800-122.pdf.

http://csrc.nist.gov/publications/nistpubs/800-66-Rev1/SP-800-66-Revision1.pdf.

http://nvlpubs.nist.gov/nistpubs/SpecialPublications/NIST.SP.800-53r4.pdf.

http://csrc.nist.gov/publications/nistpubs/800-50/NIST-SP800-50.pdf.

http://csrc.nist.gov/publications/nistpubs/800-40-Ver2/SP800-40v2.pdf.

http://csrc.nist.gov/publications/nistpubs/800-34-rev1/sp800-34-rev1_errata-Nov11-2010.pdf.

CHAPTER 5

Information Governance
and Risk Management

THIS CHAPTER WILL HELP CANDIDATES UNDERSTAND:

- Information governance
- Risk management methodology
- Key concepts associated with risk assessment
- Information risk management life cycle
- Risk management activities

INTRODUCTION

Few will disagree regarding the importance of information to healthcare organizations in their mission to provide quality patient care, conduct clinical research, and achieve business objectives. As the healthcare industry evolves to increasingly rely on digital information and technologies, so too do the nature, complexity, and volume of threats they face. Whether a global healthcare conglomerate or a small medical office, a comprehensive information governance and risk management program is a necessity whether driven by duty of care, regulatory, or legal and compliance requirements. In response to changing threat and regulatory landscapes, the healthcare industry must implement and maintain an effective information governance and risk management program. The program must be supported by knowledgeable staff and consist of reasonable administrative, physical, and technical safeguards designed to protect the confidentiality, integrity, and availability (CIA) of their information. While legal protections are mandated for certain classes of information such as personally identifiable information (PII) and personal health information (PHI) depending on where organizations conduct business, a risk-based approach for protecting all classes of information should be implemented as part of a comprehensive program.

91

Knowledge Areas

After reviewing this chapter and supporting reference materials, HCISPP candidates should comprehend the foundational principles required to implement and maintain an effective information governance and risk management program. This includes understanding how healthcare organizations manage risk through adoption of security and privacy programs, risk management methodologies, information risk management life cycle frameworks, and common risk management activities.

Industry Resources

The foundation of many information governance and risk management programs is based on common industry frameworks and standards such as those published by the National Institute of Standards and Technology (NIST), the International Organization for Standardization (ISO), and the United Kingdom's National Health Service (NHS) just to name a few. Before getting started, it is important to understand their background and some of the resources that will be referenced throughout this chapter.

National Institute of Standards and Technology

Founded in 1901, the NIST is one of the largest developers of standards and guidance within the information security field. As an agency of the US Department of Commerce, its Computer Security Division provides a broad range of information security tools, standards, and guidelines to assist with the development of risk management programs. Security resources published by NIST are generally grouped into four areas:

Federal Information Processing Standards (FIPS): Security standards surrounding compliance with the Federal Information Security Management Act (FISMA) of 2002.
NIST Special Publications (SPs): Publications from the SP 800 series (computer security) and SP 500 series (information technology) relating to computer security.
NIST Interagency or Internal Reports (NISTIRs): Background information relating to FIPS and SP publications.
Information Technology Laboratory (ITL) Bulletins: Monthly digests of NIST security publications, programs, and projects.

NIST's SPs in the 800 series are particularly useful in supporting the development of an information risk management program. Figure 5.1 provides just a few examples of the resources referenced in this chapter and the more than 150 currently published and available for free through NIST's Computer Security Resource Center (csrc.nist.gov).

Number	Title
SP 800-12	An Introduction to Computer Security: The NIST Handbook
SP 800-30 Rev. 1	Guide for Conducting Risk Assessments
SP 800-37 Rev. 1	Guide for Applying the Risk Management Framework to Federal Information Systems: A Security Lifecycle Approach
SP 800-39	Managing Information Security Risk: Organization, Mission, and Information System View
SP 800-100	Information Security Handbook: A Guide for Managers
SP 800-122	Guide to Protecting the Confidentiality of Personally Identifiable Information (PII)

FIGURE 5.1 NIST SP 800 series examples.

International Organization for Standardization

A major developer of international standards with over 19,500 published since its founding in 1947, the International Organization of Standardization (ISO) is based in Geneva, Switzerland, and its information technology standards have helped organizations build the foundation of information security programs around the world. ISO currently has members from 162 countries, thousands of technical bodies, and over 150 full-time employees supporting its development efforts. Of particular importance to security professionals and the exam are the following.

ISO/IEC 27002:2005

This information security standard was published by ISO and the International Electrotechnical Commission (IEC) under the name of *Information technology – Security techniques – Code of practice for information security management*. In layman's terms, just remember this standard is generally referred to within the industry as ISO 27002. It provides basic principles and guidance to plan, design, implement, maintain, and improve information security programs covering the following 11 knowledge areas:

- Security policy
- Organization of information security
- Asset management
- Human resources security
- Physical and environmental security
- Communications and operations management
- Access control
- Information systems acquisition, development, and maintenance
- Information security incident management
- Business continuity management
- Compliance

ISO 27799:2008

Serving as a companion to ISO/IEC 27002, this standard focuses on assisting healthcare and other organizations handling PHI implement ISO/IEC 27002 to protect the CIA of their information.

These standards are available for purchase on the ISO website: www.iso.org.

National Health Service

The United Kingdom's NHS has published an Information Governance Toolkit as a means of guiding organizations and providing a framework for implementing an information governance program. While focused on information governance, it is inclusive of information security principles and guidelines to ensure compliance with various laws including:

- The Data Protection Act 1998;
- The common law duty of confidentiality;
- The Confidentiality NHS Code of Practice;
- The NHS Care Record Guarantee for England;
- The Social Care Record Guarantee for England;
- The international information security standard: ISO/IEC 27002:2005;
- The Information Security NHS Code of Practice;
- The Records Management NHS Code of Practice;
- The Freedom of Information Act 2000;
- The Human Rights Act article 8; and
- The Code of Practice for the Management of Confidential Information.

The governance toolkit is available for free on the NHS website: www.igt.hscic.gov.uk.

UNDERSTANDING SECURITY AND PRIVACY GOVERNANCE

A strong information governance program is essential to the successful implementation of any security and privacy governance program. In the following sections, we will review the purpose of information governance and structures (frameworks) available to assist with the development of an information governance program.

Information Governance

Information governance can be defined as a structure (or framework) consisting of policies, processes, procedures, behaviors, and technologies designed to assist with managing information throughout its life cycle in a manner consistent with stakeholder expectations. The information life cycle begins when information is first created and continues until such time as the information is disposed, destroyed, or no longer requires protection. A governance structure provides an organization with the ability to manage information in a manner to help meet its business objectives while minimizing risk and maintaining compliance with the various laws where it conducts business. While information governance may have been historically viewed as a records management activity, it now requires additional stakeholder participation from areas such as human resources, finance, legal, compliance, information security, and information technology to sufficiently address a vast array of evolving cybersecurity, privacy, electronic discovery, operational, and regulatory requirements. Additionally, a key component to any information governance program includes the development and implementation of a comprehensive security and privacy program. A qualified individual must be appointed as accountable for the effective design, implementation, and continuous management of a program consisting of reasonably designed administrative, physical, and technical safeguards (also referred to as controls) to protect the CIA of its information. Administrative safeguards are defined as actions, policies, and procedures involved in the selection, development, implementation, and maintenance of security measures. These measures support the protection of information and give management guidance on the proper conduct of the workforce in relation to the protection of information. Physical safeguards are defined as physical measures to protect the organization's electronic information systems, data in physical form, buildings, and equipment from natural and environmental hazards and unauthorized intrusion. Technical safeguards are defined as the technology and associated technical standards for its use to protect and control access to information. When administrative, physical, and technical safeguards are implemented together, they can provide a strong foundation for security and privacy programs including layers of protection. While various models and resources are available to assist with developing governance structures, they all share similar principles and objectives. Prior to selecting or developing an information governance structure, it is important to establish authority, define roles and responsibilities, and engage stakeholders to solicit input and management support. After authority to build a governance program has been established, the process of defining and assigning roles and responsibilities can begin with stakeholder assistance. While roles and responsibilities will differ between organizations and various industry models, NIST SP 800-37 recommends the assignment of the following roles and responsibilities at a minimum.

Head of Agency (CEO)

The head of agency (or chief executive officer) is the highest-level official within an organization with overall responsibility for providing information security protections commensurate with the risk and magnitude of harm (i.e., impact) to organizational operations and assets, individuals, other organizations, and the Nation resulting from unauthorized access, use, disclosure, disruption, modification, or destruction of:

- Information collected or maintained by or on behalf of the agency; and
- Information systems used or operated by an agency or by a contractor of an agency or other organization on behalf of an agency.

Risk Executive (Function)

The risk executive (function) is an individual or group within an organization that helps to ensure that:

- Risk-related considerations for individual information systems, to include authorization decisions, are viewed from an organization-wide perspective with regard to the overall strategic goals and objectives of the organization in carrying out its core missions and business functions; and
- Managing information system–related security risks is consistent across the organization, reflects organizational risk tolerance, and is considered along with other types of risks in order to ensure mission/business success.

Chief Information Officer (CIO)

The CIO is an organizational official responsible for:

- Designating a senior information security officer;
- Developing and maintaining information security policies, procedures, and control techniques to address all applicable requirements;
- Overseeing personnel with significant responsibilities for information security and ensuring that the personnel are adequately trained;
- Assisting senior organizational officials concerning their security responsibilities; and
- In coordination with other senior officials, reporting annually to the head of the federal agency on the overall effectiveness of the organization's information security program, including progress of remedial actions.

Information Owner/Steward

The information owner/steward is an organizational official with statutory, management, or operational authority for specified information and the responsibility for establishing the policies and procedures governing its generation, collection, processing, dissemination, and disposal. In information-sharing environments, the information owner/steward is responsible for establishing the rules for appropriate use and protection of the subject information (e.g., rules of behavior) and retains that responsibility even when the information is shared with or provided to other organizations. The owner/steward of the information processed, stored, or transmitted by an information system may or may not be the same as the system owner. A single information system may contain information from multiple information owners/stewards. Information owners/stewards provide input to information system owners regarding the security requirements and security controls for the systems where the information is processed, stored, or transmitted.

Senior Information Security Officer

The senior information security officer, also known as Chief Information Security Officer (CISO) or Chief Security Officer (CSO), is an organizational official responsible for:

- Carrying out the CIO security responsibilities under FISMA; and
- Serving as the primary liaison for the CIO to the organization's authorizing officials, information system owners, common control providers, and information system security officers.

The senior information security officer:

- Possesses professional qualifications, including training and experience, required to administer the information security program functions;
- Maintains information security duties as a primary responsibility; and
- Heads an office with the mission and resources to assist the organization in achieving more secure information and information systems in accordance with the requirements in FISMA.

Authorizing Official

The authorizing official is a senior official or executive with the authority to formally assume responsibility for operating an information system at an acceptable level of risk to organizational operations and assets, individuals, other organizations, and the Nation. Authorizing officials typically have budgetary oversight for an information system or are responsible for the mission and/or business operations supported by the system. Through the security authorization process, authorizing officials are accountable for the security risks associated with information system operations. Accordingly, authorizing officials are in management positions with a level of authority commensurate with understanding and accepting such information system–related security risks. Authorizing officials:

- Approve security plans, memorandums of agreement or understanding, and plans of action and milestones and determine whether significant changes in the information systems or environments of operation require reauthorization;
- Deny authorization to operate an information system or if the system is operational, halt operations, if unacceptable risks exist;
- Coordinate their activities with the risk executive (function), CIO, senior information security officer, common control providers, information system owners, information system security officers, security control assessors, and other interested parties during the security authorization process; and
- Are responsible for ensuring that all activities and functions associated with security authorization that are delegated to authorizing official designated representatives are carried out.

Authorizing Official Designated Representative

The authorizing official designated representative is an organizational official who acts on behalf of an authorizing official to coordinate and conduct the required day-to-day activities associated with the security authorization process. Authorizing official designated representatives can be:

- Empowered by authorizing officials to make certain decisions with regard to the planning and resourcing of the security authorization process, approval of the security plan, approval and monitoring of the implementation of plans of action and milestones, and the assessment and/or determination of risk; and
- Called upon to prepare the final authorization package, obtain the authorizing official's signature on the authorization decision document, and transmit the authorization package to appropriate organizational officials.

Common Control Provider

The common control provider is an individual, group, or organization responsible for the development, implementation, assessment, and monitoring of common controls (i.e., security controls inherited by information systems). Common control providers are responsible for:

- Documenting the organization-identified common controls in a security plan (or equivalent document prescribed by the organization);
- Ensuring that required assessments of common controls are carried out by qualified assessors with an appropriate level of independence defined by the organization;
- Documenting assessment findings in a security assessment report; and
- Producing a plan of action and milestones for all controls having weaknesses or deficiencies.

Information System Owner

The information system owner is an organizational official responsible for the procurement, development, integration, modification, operation, maintenance, and disposal of an information system. The information system owner is responsible for:

- Addressing the operational interests of the user community (i.e., users who require access to the information system to satisfy mission, business, or operational requirements);
- Ensuring compliance with information security requirements;
- In coordination with the information system security officer, development and maintenance of the security plan and ensuring that the system is deployed and operated in accordance with the agreed-upon security controls; and

- In coordination with the information owner/steward, deciding who has access to the system (and with what types of privileges or access rights) and ensuring that system users and support personnel receive the requisite security training (e.g., instruction in rules of behavior).

Information System Security Officer

The information system security officer is an individual responsible for ensuring that the appropriate operational security posture is maintained for an information system and, as such, works in close collaboration with the information system owner. The information system security officer:

- Serves as a principal advisor on all matters, technical and otherwise, involving the security of an information system;
- Has detailed knowledge and expertise required to manage the security aspects of an information system and, in many organizations, is assigned responsibility for the day-to-day security operations of a system;
- May be called upon to assist in the development of the security policies and procedures and to ensure compliance with those policies and procedures; and
- In close coordination with the information system owner, often plays an active role in the monitoring of a system and its environment of operation to include developing and updating the security plan, managing and controlling changes to the system, and assessing the security impact of those changes.

Information Security Architect

The information security architect is an individual, group, or organization responsible for ensuring that the information security requirements necessary to protect the organization's core missions and business processes are adequately addressed in all aspects of enterprise architecture including reference models, segment and solution architectures, and the resulting information systems supporting those missions and business processes. The information security architect:

- Serves as the liaison between the enterprise architect and the information system security engineer;
- Coordinates with information system owners, common control providers, and information system security officers on the allocation of security controls as system-specific, hybrid, or common controls; and
- In close coordination with information system security officers, advises authorizing officials, CIOs, senior information security officers, and the risk executive (function), on a range of security-related issues including, for example, establishing information system boundaries, assessing the

severity of weaknesses and deficiencies in the information system, plans of action and milestones, risk mitigation approaches, security alerts, and potential adverse effects of identified vulnerabilities.

Information System Security Engineer

The information system security engineer is an individual, group, or organization responsible for conducting information system security engineering activities. Information system security engineering is a process that captures and refines information security requirements and ensures that the requirements are effectively integrated into information technology component products and information systems through purposeful security architecting, design, development, and configuration. Information system security engineers:

- Serve as an integral part of the development team (e.g., integrated project team) designing and developing organizational information systems or upgrading legacy systems;
- Employ best practices when implementing security controls within an information system including software engineering methodologies, system/security engineering principles, secure design, secure architecture, and secure coding techniques; and
- Coordinate their security-related activities with information security architects, senior information security officers, information system owners, common control providers, and information system security officers.

Security Control Assessor

The security control assessor is an individual, group, or organization responsible for conducting a comprehensive assessment of the management, operational, and technical security controls employed within or inherited by an information system to determine the overall effectiveness of the controls (i.e., the extent to which the controls are implemented correctly, operating as intended, and producing the desired outcome with respect to meeting the security requirements for the system). Security control assessors:

- Provide an assessment of the severity of weaknesses or deficiencies discovered in the information system and its environment of operation and recommend corrective actions to address identified vulnerabilities; and
- Prepare the final security assessment report containing the results and findings from the assessment.

Governance Structures

For purposes of the exam and understanding the basic principles and objectives involved, next we will review the governance structures published by the NIST and the United Kingdom's NHS.

NIST Structure

The NIST SP 800-39 outlines three approaches (centralized, decentralized, and hybrid) to information security governance. The approaches differ in authority, responsibility, and decision-making power and selecting an appropriate structure will vary based on a number of factors (e.g., business requirements, organization culture and size, risk tolerance). However, the information security governance structures are aligned with other governance structures (e.g., information technology governance) to maximize compatibility and overall effectiveness.

Centralized Governance

In centralized governance structures, the authority, responsibility, and decision-making power are vested solely within central bodies. These centralized bodies establish the appropriate policies, procedures, and processes for ensuring organization-wide involvement in the development and implementation of risk management and information security strategies, risk, and information security decisions, and the creation of interorganizational and intraorganizational communication mechanisms. A centralized approach to governance requires strong, well-informed central leadership and provides consistency throughout the organization. Centralized governance structures also provide less autonomy for subordinate organizations that are part of the parent organization.

Decentralized Governance

In decentralized information security governance structures, the authority, responsibility, and decision-making power are vested in and delegated to individual subordinate organizations within the parent organization (e.g., bureaus/components within an executive department of the federal government or business units within a corporation). Subordinate organizations establish their own policies, procedures, and processes for ensuring (sub) organization-wide involvement in the development and implementation of risk management and information security strategies, risk and information security decisions, and the creation of mechanisms to communicate within the organization. A decentralized approach to information security governance accommodates subordinate organizations with divergent mission/business needs and operating environments at the cost of consistency throughout the organization as a whole. The effectiveness of this approach is greatly increased by the sharing of risk-related information among subordinate organizations so that no subordinate organization is able to transfer risk to another without the latter's informed consent. It is also important to share risk-related information with parent organizations as the risk decisions by subordinate organizations may have an effect on the organization as a whole.

Hybrid Governance

In hybrid information security governance structures, the authority, responsibility, and decision-making power are distributed between a central body and individual subordinate organizations. The central body establishes the policies, procedures, and processes for ensuring organization-wide involvement in the portion of the risk management and information security strategies and decisions affecting the entire organization (e.g., decisions related to shared infrastructure or common security services). Subordinate organizations, in a similar manner, establish appropriate policies, procedures, and processes for ensuring their involvement in the portion of the risk management and information security strategies and decisions that are specific to their mission/business needs and environments of operation. A hybrid approach to governance requires strong, well-informed leadership for the organization as a whole and for subordinate organizations, and provides consistency throughout the organization for those aspects of risk and information security that affect the entire organization.

National Health Service Structure

As an alternate framework, the United Kingdom's NHS has published an information governance toolkit (the "NHS Toolkit") designed to enable organizations and partners to assess compliance with the various laws, policies, and standards associated with information governance. While this particular toolkit incorporates legal requirements for healthcare organizations operating in the United Kingdom, it provides foundational principles that should be part of any information governance program and can be adapted to incorporate requirements for healthcare organizations operating in any jurisdiction. The NHS Toolkit provides a framework of information governance requirements inclusive of security and privacy objectives that vary by the type of healthcare organization. As an example, the minimum requirements for General Practice organizations cover the three control areas shown in Figure 5.2: information governance management, confidentiality and data protection assurance, and information security assurance.

FIGURE 5.2 NHS General Practice information governance life cycle.

Req No	Description
Information Governance Management	
11-114	Responsibility for Information Governance has been assigned to an appropriate member, or members, of staff
11-115	There is an information governance policy that addresses the overall requirements of information governance
11-116	All contracts (staff, contractor and third party) contain clauses that clearly identify information governance responsibilities
11-117	All staff members are provided with appropriate training on information governance requirements
Confidentiality and Data Protection Assurance	
11-211	All transfers of personal and sensitive information are conducted in a secure and confidential manner
11-212	Consent is appropriately sought before personal information is used in ways that do not directly contribute to the delivery of care services and objections to the disclosure of confidential personal information are appropriately respected
11-213	There is a publicly available and easy to understand information leaflet that informs patients/service users how their information is used, who may have access to that information, and their own rights to see and obtain copies of their records
Information Security Assurance	
11-304	Monitoring and enforcement processes are in place to ensure NHS national application Smartcard users comply with the terms and conditions of use
11-316	There is an information asset register that includes all key information, software, hardware and services
11-317	Unauthorized access to the premises, equipment, records and other assets is prevented
11-318	The use of mobile computing systems is controlled, monitored and audited to ensure their correct operation and to prevent unauthorized access
11-319	There are documented plans and procedures to support business continuity in the event of power failures, system failures, natural disasters and other disruptions
11-320	There are documented incident management and reporting procedures

FIGURE 5.3 Minimum requirements for General Practice organizations.

While Figure 5.2 provides a high-level overview of the requirements for General Practice organizations, requirements for alternate types of healthcare organizations are available on the NHS Toolkit website (www.igt.hscic.gov.uk). The NHS Toolkit also provides the minimum requirements for each control area as shown in Figure 5.3 based on the various laws and policies governing a General Practice organization. Additional supplemental assessment and implementation guidance for each individual control is available on the NHS Toolkit website.

UNDERSTANDING RISK MANAGEMENT METHODOLOGY

A comprehensive risk management methodology is a foundational component to any successful security and privacy program, and is driven by regulatory requirements in many jurisdictions. For example, the HIPAA Security Rule requires organizations to implement policies and procedures to prevent, detect, contain, and correct security violations with risk analysis as one of the four required implementation specifications. It also requires organizations to conduct accurate and thorough assessments of the potential risks and vulnerabilities to the CIA of electronic protected health information. Risk assessments

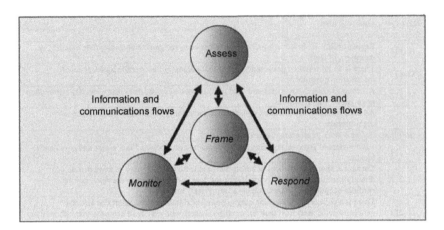

FIGURE 5.4 NIST risk assessment within the risk management process.

should be conducted on a periodic basis and designed to identify, assess, prioritize, respond to, and monitor risk to the organization for the purpose of informing and enabling stakeholders to make risk-based decisions. The methods for risk analysis will vary based on the size, complexity, and capabilities of an organization, but for purposes of the exam we will focus on the important concepts and steps involved in a risk management methodology including preparation, execution, communication, and maintenance as recommended by NIST (Figure 5.4).

Framing
The first component of the risk management methodology involves understanding the environment in which the organization operates and its risk tolerance (or appetite) to ensure risk is appropriately framed. The purpose of framing is to enable implementation of a risk management strategy that aligns with how an organization plans to assess, respond to, and monitor risk based on their established risk tolerance and decision-making processes. This provides the framework for managing risk and enabling risk-based decisions.

Assessment
The second component of the methodology involves assessing risk to identify threats, vulnerabilities, potential impact (harm) and likelihood harm will occur for the purpose of determining risk.

Response
The third component of the methodology addresses how an organization should respond to risk once identified. It also ensures alignment with the organization's risk management strategy, evaluation of options for risk acceptance, avoidance,

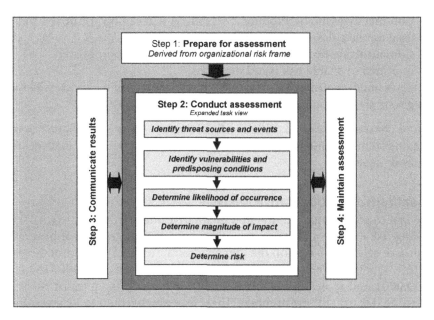

FIGURE 5.5 NIST risk assessment process.

remediation and transfer, determination of appropriate courses of action, and successful implementation of actions in accordance with risk decision.

Monitoring

The final component of the risk methodology involves the monitoring of risk over time for the purpose of evaluating control effectiveness, identifying system and environment changes that create risk, and ensuring risk responses are implemented in alignment with business objectives, regulatory requirements, and security and privacy policies, standards, and guidelines. Risk management methodologies can be incorporated into a number of risk processes and activities to assist with development of an information security architecture, defining requirements for the interconnection of information systems, designing security controls and supporting implementation of information systems and various technologies, access management processes and authorization controls, and valuation of changes to information systems.

Risk Assessment Approach

The high-level steps involved in a risk assessment as outlined by the NIST SP 800-30 are (Figure 5.5):

  Assessment preparation: Establish a context for the assessment informed by risk framing as discussed earlier.

Conduct assessment: Produce a list of risks that can be prioritized and used to make risk-based decisions.

Communicate results: Ensure decision makers are appropriately informed to enable risk-based decisions.

Assessment maintenance: Monitor changes and ensure risk assessment results are kept up to date.

Before discussing the information risk assessment process in Chapter 6, it is first important to understand key concepts associated with risk management methodologies.

Quantitative and Qualitative Analysis

The first concept is quantitative and qualitative analysis. An approach for assessing risk can be qualitative, quantitative, or a combination of both with approach selection based on the organization's existing risk methodology or culture. Quantitative assessments involve numbers (e.g., $10,000, $50,000, $100,000) and typically involve a set of methods, principles, or rules for assessing risk using these numbers. These assessments tend to be less subjective than other methods and are quite effective when evaluating the costs and benefits of various risk responses to assist decision makers in selecting an appropriate course of action. However, the results are not always straightforward after taking into consideration potential assumptions and constraints associated with the results, so interpretation and further explanation may be required. The quality of a quantitative assessment can be measured by the rigor, repeatability, and reproducibility of the results, but sometimes outweighed by the cost associated with obtaining the results due to the time and expertise required. Quantitative assessments can also be measured in terms of:

Single loss expectancy (SLE): Loss in monetary (e.g., dollars) terms associated with occurrence of a single event. Expressed as an equation: SLE = asset value × exposure (% of loss of total asset value).

Annual rate of occurrence (ARO): The anticipated frequency that a SLE event is projected to occur in a 12-month period.

Annual loss expectancy (ALE): The expected loss over a 12-month period based on the SLE of an event and the ARO. Expressed as an equation: ALE = SLE × ARO.

For example, let us say an organization has 10,000 records of electronic PHI including names and Social Security numbers stored within an application. If we can tie the total potential loss of each health record to a specific dollar figure such as $200, the maximum potential impact in a situation where all records are lost would not exceed $2,000,000. If a particular event occurs twice

	Risk		
	Low	Moderate	High
Media coverage	Local	Regional	National

FIGURE 5.6 Qualitative analysis based on media coverage.

every 12 months and results in a 5% loss of records per event, we can calculate the following:

Maximum impact ($2,000,000) = records (10,000) × impact ($200 per record)
SLE ($100,000) = asset value ($2,000,000) × exposure (5%)
ALE ($200,000) = SLE ($100,000) × ARO (2 per year)

Alternatively, qualitative assessments involve non-numerical categories or levels (e.g., low, moderate, high) and can be more effective when communicating with stakeholders. However, this type of analysis is subjective and each category or level must be clearly defined to produce results that are repeatable and reproducible. Similar to quantitative, further explanation may be required including the summarization of reasons supporting the result. For example, let us say we want to measure an organization's risk associated with losing 10,000 records of electronic PHI in terms of how much media coverage it receives. While we may be unable to quantify the loss in dollars, it can be expressed in categorical terms if associated with each type of media coverage (Figure 5.6).

If the organization received regional media coverage associated with the loss of these 10,000 records (moderate impact) and we estimate this loss would occur every 5 years (likelihood), a qualitative approach using Figure 5.7 would conclude this presents an overall medium risk to the organization.

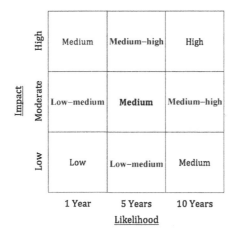

FIGURE 5.7 Qualitative analysis leveraging likelihood and impact.

Asset Identification and Valuation

The second concept to understand involves asset identification and valuation. An important component to a risk management methodology is the identification and inventory of information assets. Without an accurate asset inventory, it will be difficult to assess risk and ensure appropriate administrative, physical, and technical safeguards are implemented to protect the organization's assets. For example, as the HIPAA Security Rule mandates protection for electronic protected health information, the organization must understand where this type of information is stored, received, maintained, or transmitted to ensure it receives appropriate protections and the organization maintains compliance with the law. Asset valuation is another important factor in identifying the importance of assets to an organization. Value can be derived in both tangible and intangible forms and associated with risk (e.g., low, medium, high). Tangible forms involve direct (real) value of physical assets including revenue and server or facility costs. Intangible forms involve indirect value such as brand, reputation, and loss of prospective customers and intellectual property. For example, let us say a healthcare organization has an online prescription filling system that generates $5000 per hour in revenue. If the system goes offline unexpectedly for 3 hours and leaves the organization unable to take new orders or fill prescriptions, the organization would have $15,000 in tangible (direct) revenue losses. The organization might also incur intangible losses associated with media coverage of the outage impacting brand and reputation or customers filling prescriptions with a competitor. An inventory of information assets and their associated value will enable organizations to leverage a risk-based approach to protecting only those assets with the greatest need of protection. Otherwise organizations will be left wasting resources and likely failing to protect all information assets equally based on the highest set of requirements.

Threats

The next concept to understand is a threat, which is any event with the potential to adversely impact the CIA of information systems through unauthorized access, destruction, disclosure, or modification of information, or denial of service. Healthcare organizations will need to identify threats that are unique and reasonably applicable to their operating environment. Threat sources can be internal or external and involve:

- Hostile cyber or physical attacks
- Structure failures of organization-controlled resources (e.g., hardware, software)
- Natural or man-made disasters and accidents (even intentional)

Internal threats involve resources (e.g., employees, contractors, vendors) with access to the organization's assets and threats can even come from the assets themselves. These can include:

- An internal contractor attempting unauthorized access to an information system, posing a threat to data confidentiality
- An employee accidently entering the wrong Social Security number for a patient, posing a threat to data integrity
- A backup generator for the organization's data center failing to start during a power outage, posing a threat to availability

External threats are those from sources outside the organization's control such as weather (e.g., hurricanes, tornados, floods) resulting in a natural disaster or cyber attacks conducted by organized crime rings.

Vulnerability

The next concept to understand is vulnerability (sometimes referred to as exposure), which can be characterized as any weakness in an information system such as servers, networks, and infrastructure that could be intentionally or unintentionally exploited by a threat. While many can be attributed to the absence or ineffectiveness of security controls, some arise naturally due to changes in people, process, and technology over time. Healthcare organizations must identify vulnerabilities, which, if exploited by a threat, reasonably present a risk of inappropriate access to or disclosure of PHI. Examples of vulnerabilities may include:

System patching: As server, network, and infrastructure vulnerabilities are identified, manufacturers typically release software patches to fix or mitigate the vulnerability. If organizations have not implemented effective patching processes, they will remain exposed to these vulnerabilities and provide threats an opportunity to exploit them.

System hardening: Systems should be sufficiently hardened to provide additional security beyond base or default configurations. This includes disabling or removing unnecessary services and software, changing default passwords and administrator accounts, and ensuring appropriate patches are applied. Without effective hardening practices, systems will be exposed to a greater number of vulnerabilities over time and will increase the opportunity for threats to exploit them.

Mobile media: Organizations should control the use of mobile media devices such as USB storage devices. These devices can introduce malicious software directly onto an information system or provide a means for information to be copied off of the organization's systems.

Backup: Information and systems should be regularly backed up to enable the organization to recover from an adverse event. If a system vulnerability were exploited by a threat or encountered due to a natural disaster and resulted in the corruption or loss of data, an organization will need to be able to sufficiently recover using backup processes and procedures.

Administrative	Physical	Technical
Policies	Walls	Firewalls
Standards	Barriers	Antivirus software
Processes	Fences	Encryption
Procedures	Doors	Authentication
Guidelines	Guards	Software patching

FIGURE 5.8 Control examples.

Change management: Vulnerabilities can be introduced by changes in people, process, and technology. An effective change management process can include the evaluation of potential impacts resulting from a change and ensure vulnerabilities are sufficiently mitigated prior to change implementation.

Access management: Inappropriate access to systems, networks, and infrastructure introduces vulnerabilities for threat exploitation. If the user account of a terminated contractor is not removed or disabled in a timely manner, the account could facilitate unauthorized access.

Controls

The next concept to understand is controls, which are techniques, methods, policies, standards, processes, procedures, guidelines, and physical devices designed to mitigate the vulnerability of an information asset or probability of successful vulnerability exploitation by a threat. Controls are also referred to as safeguards and can be administrative, physical, or technical in nature to reduce an organization's exposure to both threats and vulnerabilities. Figure 5.8 provides examples of various administrative, physical, and technical controls.

Likelihood

The next concept to understand is likelihood, which is an estimate of the likelihood (also referred to as probability) a threat will be motivated and capable of exploiting a vulnerability. It addresses the probability or possibility that an event will occur and result in an adverse impact, regardless of the magnitude of harm that is expected. The estimation should be determined based on current state of the target system, an analysis of existing control effectiveness, and the expected likelihood after new controls are applied. Likelihood should also be associated with a specific time frame (e.g., next month, 6 months, 1 year, 5 years) and take into consideration the estimated frequency of an event. Figure 5.9 provides an example of likelihood associated with frequency.

Likelihood	Frequency
Low	Occurs once per 5 years
Moderate	Occurs once per 1 year
High	Occurs once per 6 months

FIGURE 5.9 Association between likelihood and frequency.

As part of the estimation process, organizations should assess the likelihood a threat will attempt to exploit one or more vulnerabilities and the likelihood it will result in an adverse impact or harm the organization.

Impact

The next concept to understand is impact, which is the expected harm or damage to an organization resulting from the successful exploitation of a vulnerability. The harm or damage can result from unauthorized information disclosure, modification, destruction, or loss of availability and be realized by both organizational and nonorganizational stakeholders such as clients, shareholders, business heads, or information system owners. Some organizations may define how established values and priorities guide the identification of important assets and the potential adverse impact to organizational stakeholders using a process generally referred to as asset classification. This process enables an organization to clearly indicate the organizational impact associated with different types of information. Figure 5.10 provides an example of asset classification where impacts are associated with specific data types.

Risk

The next concept to understand is risk, which is a measure of the extent to which an organization is threatened by a particular event. It is also a function of the likelihood the adverse event occurs and the resulting impact to the organization. One of the more common ways to express risk is using a formula as follows:

Risk = threat × vulnerability

Several lower-level risks can also be aggregated (combined) into one general or higher-level risk. For example, if an assessment produces four low and two medium risks, they could be reflected as one high (medium + medium) and one medium (low + low + low + low) when aggregated together depending on the nature of the risks involved.

There are three main types of risk: inherent, managed, and residual. Inherent risk is the maximum potential loss and likelihood associated with a particular event given the absence of controls or safeguards. Managed (also referred to as

Classification	Low	Moderate	High
Information type	Public information marketing materials	Internal information Policies, Processes-and procedures	Electronic patient health informtion non public personal information organization financials
Impact	Unexpected financial loss less than $1k Local media coverage No regulatory findings Small impact to operations	Unexpected financial loss between $1 and 10k Regional media coverage Minor regulatory findings Medium impact to operations	Unexpected financial loss greater than $10k National media coverage Major regulatory findings Large impact to operations

FIGURE 5.10 Example of asset classification.

FIGURE 5.11 Risk types and relationships.

mitigated) risk is the potential loss and likelihood associated with a particular event with existing controls and safeguards in place. Residual risk is the potential loss and likelihood remaining after existing and newly proposed controls, safeguards, and actions have been implemented. Figure 5.11 provides an overview of how these three risk types interrelate.

Risk Treatment
Organizations generally have four possible options for responding to different types of risks that include:

- **Acceptance**: Decision to accept a particular risk and its associated losses assuming it falls within an organization's risk tolerance. Acceptance usually occurs for lower risks or when the cost associated with selecting one of the other three options exceeds the maximum potential loss of the asset.
- **Transfer**: Decision to fully or partially transfer a particular risk and its associated losses to a third party such as vendor or insurance company. For example, if the maximum potential loss associated with an asset is $100,000, an organization might purchase a $75,000 insurance policy from a third party to reduce its direct risk exposure to $25,000 (after insurance coverage).
- **Mitigate**: Decision to reduce vulnerabilities through implementation of additional administrative, physical, and/or technical safeguards. For example, to reduce the risk of data loss associated with a lost or stolen laptop, an organization might implement encryption as an additional technical control.
- **Avoid**: Decision to avoid taking actions or activities that would create new risk for the organization. For example, if implementation of a new website would provide $100,000 in revenue but result in $500,000 in risk exposure on an annual basis, an organization may choose to avoid the risk altogether by not implementing the new website in the first place.

INFORMATION RISK MANAGEMENT LIFE CYCLE AND ACTIVITIES

Information risk management is a continuous life cycle beginning from the point information is created and ending when information is disposed, destroyed, or no longer requires protection. While various frameworks have been

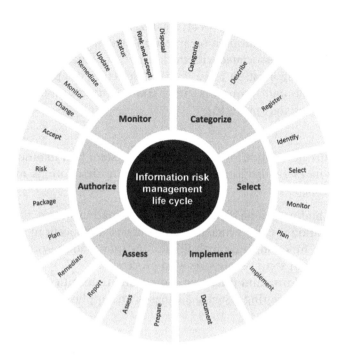

FIGURE 5.12 Information risk management life cycle.

published by the Centers for Medicare & Medicaid Services (CMS), ISO, and NIST, all share similar principles and objectives. For purposes of the exam and understanding the basic principles and objectives of information risk management life cycles and associated activities, we will focus on the NIST SP 800-37 framework as shown in Figure 5.12.

A system development life cycle typically involves five phases including initiation (concept/requirements definition), development/acquisition, implementation, operation/maintenance, and disposal. Each risk management life cycle step shown in Figure 5.12 is integrated into each system development life cycle phase.

Step 1: Categorize Information Systems

The categorization of information systems involves three distinct tasks that occur during the initiation stage of the system development life cycle. This step also assists with the identification of assets and information systems that create, receive, transmit, or maintain electronic PHI as required by the HIPAA Security Rule.

Categorize

Arguably the most important item is the implementation of a security categorization process that ensures information systems are categorized based on the mission and business objectives of an organization. The categorization process also takes into consideration an organization's risk management strategy and the potential impact associated with the loss of CIA of the information system. The results of categorization assist with the selection of appropriate administrative, physical, and technical security controls to ensure the information system is appropriately protected.

Describe

Document the description of the information system in a manner commensurate with its categorization. Information system descriptions may include information such as:

- Name and/or unique identifier of the information system;
- Information system owner, relevant contacts, and location;
- Purpose, function, and capabilities of the information system;
- Results from security categorization process;
- Types of information processed, stored, and transmitted; and/or
- Hardware, operating systems, databases, and applications involved.

Register

Include the information system within the organization's system inventory and define who will own, manage, and/or control the system. When all tasks are completed, the system owner should be able to answer in the affirmative to the checkpoint questions in Figure 5.13.

Step 2: Select Security Controls

The selection of security controls step involves four distinct tasks that occur during the initiation or development/acquisition stages of the system development life cycle.

Identify

Identify common security controls that are provided by the organization and inherited by information systems during the initiation stage of the development

---

Milestone Checkpoint #1

- Has the organization completed a *security categorization* of the information system (informed by the initial risk assessment) including the information to be processed, stored, and transmitted by the system?
- Are the results of the security categorization process for the information system consistent with the organization's *enterprise architecture* and commitment to *protecting organizational mission/business processes*?
- Do the results of the security categorization process reflect the organization's *risk management strategy*?
- Has the organization adequately described the *characteristics* of the information system?
- Has the organization *registered* the information system for purposes of management, accountability, coordination, and oversight?

FIGURE 5.13 NIST step 1 checkpoint.

life cycle. If common controls will not be sufficient to adequately protect an information system, the system owner will need to evaluate system-specific controls or risk acceptance as possible options.

Select

Select, tailor, and document the required security controls based on the information system's categorization during the initiation phase of the system development life cycle. Risk assessment results can also be leveraged to provide guidance during the security control selection process. After selection is completed, security controls may need to be tailored so they more closely align with the needs of the organization or information system. The tailoring process generally involves establishing baseline security controls, adjusting baseline controls and selecting additional compensating controls where necessary, and providing guidance for control implementation.

Monitor

Develop a strategy to continuously monitor security control effectiveness during the initiation phase of the system development life cycle. After controls are implemented, an important component of any risk management program is monitoring effectiveness of the control to understand the state of the information system over time as a result of evolving threats, vulnerabilities, technologies, and business objectives. Criteria are also defined and agreed to by the system owner to determine the frequency with which security controls are assessed and monitored postdeployment.

Plan

Develop, review, and approve an overall information system security plan during the development/acquisition phase of the system development life cycle. The system owner and other appropriate stakeholders review the security plan to ensure it is complete and consistent, and satisfies the security requirements for the information system. If no changes are required, the plan is accepted and the system owner should be able to answer in the affirmative to the checkpoint questions in Figure 5.14.

Acceptance of the security plan represents an important milestone in both the risk management process and the system development life cycle. The stakeholder, by approving the security plan, agrees to the set of security controls proposed to meet the security requirements for the information system. This approval allows the risk management process to advance to the next step in the RMF (i.e., the implementation of the security controls). The approval of the security plan also establishes the level of effort required to successfully complete the remainder of the steps in the RMF and provides the basis of the security specification for the acquisition of the information system, subsystems, or components.

Milestone Checkpoint #2

- Has the organization allocated all security controls to the *information system* as system-specific, hybrid, or common controls?
- Has the organization used its *risk assessment* (either formal or informal) to inform and guide the security control selection process?
- Has the organization identified *authorizing officials* for the information system and all common controls inherited by the system?
- Has the organization *tailored* the baseline security controls to ensure that the controls, if implemented, adequately mitigate risks to organizational operations and assets, individuals, other organizations, and the Nation?
- Has the organization addressed *minimum assurance requirements* for the security controls employed within and inherited by the information system?
- Has the organization consulted information system owners when *identifying common controls* to ensure that the security capability provided by the inherited controls is sufficient to deliver adequate protection?
- Has the organization *supplemented* the *common controls* with system-specific or hybrid controls when the security control baselines of the common controls are less than those of the information system inheriting the controls?
- Has the organization documented the common controls inherited from *external providers*?
- Has the organization developed a *continuous monitoring strategy* for the information system (including monitoring of security control effectiveness for system-specific, hybrid, and common controls) that reflects the organizational risk management strategy and organizational commitment to protecting critical missions and business functions?
- Have appropriate organizational officials *approved* security plans containing system-specific, hybrid, and common controls?

FIGURE 5.14 NIST step 2 checkpoint.

Step 3: Implement Security Controls

The implementation of security controls step involves two distinct tasks that occur during both the development/acquisition and implementation stages of the system development life cycle.

Implement

Implement the security controls defined by the security plan in a manner consistent with the organization's enterprise and information security architecture and industry best practice. A security engineering process should be invoked to evaluate the control requirements and assist with their design and integration into information systems.

Document

Document how the security controls were implemented as part of the security plan. Documentation should include expectations regarding overall information system performance, details surrounding the implementation of common and system-specific administrative, physical, and technical security controls, and any system or platform dependencies. When all tasks are completed, the system owner should be able to answer in the affirmative to the checkpoint questions in Figure 5.15.

Step 4: Assess Security Controls

The assessment of security controls step involves four distinct tasks that occur during both the development/acquisition and implementation stages of the system development life cycle.

> **Milestone Checkpoint #3**
>
> - Has the organization *allocated* security controls as system-specific, hybrid, or common controls consistent with the enterprise architecture and information security architecture?
> - Has the organization demonstrated the use of sound *information system and security engineering methodologies* in integrating information technology products into the information system and in implementing the security controls contained in the security plan?
> - Has the organization documented how *common controls* inherited by organizational information systems have been implemented?
> - Has the organization documented how *system-specific* and *hybrid* security controls have been implemented within the information system taking into account specific technologies and platform dependencies?
> - Has the organization taken into account the *minimum assurance requirements* when implementing security controls?

FIGURE 5.15 NIST step 3 checkpoint.

Prepare

Develop, review, and approve a security assessment plan that defines objectives, road map for a security controls assessment, and assessment procedures. The plan should also ensure the individual performing the assessment (assessor) has sufficient technical expertise and independence (no conflicts of interest) to successfully carry out the assessment.

Assess

Execute the security assessment plan to determine if controls are implemented correctly, operating as intended, and producing the desired outcome to meet the information systems security requirements. The assessment should be performed early in the system development life cycle to enable identified security weaknesses and deficiencies to be resolved in a more cost-effective and timely manner. The assessor will be responsible for evaluating the security controls in accordance with the assessment procedure and providing the information system owner with specific recommendations on how to correct security control weaknesses or deficiencies and reduce or eliminate vulnerabilities.

Report

Prepare the security assessment report that includes details with regard to issues, findings, recommendations, and information pertaining to overall security control effectiveness.

Remediate

Begin initial remediation (or treatment) of issues and findings and reassessment of remediated controls. If information system owners and management decide that certain findings warrant immediate action, they may direct that initial remediation begin immediately. After initial remediation has completed, the assessor will need to reevaluate the remediated controls and update the assessment report where appropriate. Once the assessment has been completed, the security plan should also be updated to ensure it includes a list

Milestone Checkpoint #4

- Has the organization developed a comprehensive *plan* to assess the security controls employed within or inherited by the information system?
- Was the assessment plan *reviewed* and *approved* by appropriate organizational officials?
- Has the organization considered the appropriate level of assessor *independence* for the security control assessment?
- Has the organization provided all of the essential supporting *assessment-related materials* needed by the assessor(s) to conduct an effective security control assessment?
- Has the organization examined opportunities for *reusing assessment results* from previous assessments or from other sources?
- Did the assessor(s) complete the *security control assessment* in accordance with the stated assessment plan?
- Did the organization receive the completed *security assessment report* with appropriate findings and recommendations from the assessor(s)?
- Did the organization take the necessary *remediation actions* to address the most important weaknesses and deficiencies in the information system and its environment of operation based on the findings and recommendations in the security assessment report?
- Did the assessor *reassess the remediated controls* for effectiveness to provide the authorization official with an unbiased, factual security assessment report on the weaknesses or deficiencies in the system?
- Did the organization update appropriate *security plans* based on the findings and recommendations in the security assessment report and any subsequent changes to the information system and its environment of operation?

FIGURE 5.16 NIST step 4 checkpoint.

and description of implemented security controls and residual vulnerabilities. When all tasks are completed, the system owner should be able to answer in the affirmative to the checkpoint questions in Figure 5.16.

Step 5: Authorize Information System

The authorization of information systems step involves four distinct tasks that occur during the implementation stage of the system development life cycle.

Plan

Prepare a plan of action and associated milestones based on the findings and recommendations from the security assessment report.

Package

Prepare and submit the security plan, security assessment report, and plan of action as a package to management for review.

Risk

Determine the overall risk to the organization's operations based on its risk management methodology and evaluate potential courses of action including risk acceptance, avoidance, mitigation, or transfer.

Accept

Determine if the risk is acceptable and provide authorization to the system owner including terms, conditions, and end date where appropriate. When all

Milestone Checkpoint #5

- Did the organization develop a *plan of action and milestones* reflecting organizational priorities for addressing the remaining weaknesses and deficiencies in the information system and its environment of operation?
- Did the organization develop an appropriate *authorization package* with all key documents including the security plan, security assessment report, and plan of action and milestones (if applicable)?
- Did the final *risk determination* and *risk acceptance* by the authorizing official reflect the risk management strategy developed by the organization and conveyed by the risk executive (function)?
- Was the *authorization decision* conveyed to appropriate organizational personnel including information system owners and common control providers?

FIGURE 5.17 NIST step 5 checkpoint.

tasks are completed, the system owner should be able to answer in the affirmative to the checkpoint questions in Figure 5.17.

Step 6: Monitoring Security Controls

The monitoring of security controls step involves seven distinct tasks that occur during the operation/maintenance or disposal stages of the system development life cycle.

System Change

Assess the security impact associated with proposed or actual changes to the information system and its operating environment during the operation/maintenance stage of the development life cycle. As information systems are in a constant state of change, a formal process to assess, manage, control, and document information system changes is required to monitor and ensure security controls remain effective.

Monitor

Implement continuous monitoring of information system operational and technical security controls based on the approved security plan during the operation/maintenance stage of the development life cycle.

Remediate

Remediate issues and deficiencies identified from continuous monitoring, risk assessments, and any remaining action plans during the operation/maintenance stage of the development life cycle.

Update

Regularly update the security plan, assessment report, and plan of action during the operation/maintenance stage of the development life cycle based on results of continuous monitoring and progress toward issue and deficiency remediation.

Milestone Checkpoint #6
- Is the organization effectively monitoring changes to the *information system* and its *environment of operation* including the effectiveness of deployed *security controls* in accordance with the continuous monitoring strategy?
- Is the organization effectively analyzing the *security impacts* of identified changes to the information system and its environment of operation?
- Is the organization conducting *ongoing assessments of security controls* in accordance with the monitoring strategy?
- Is the organization taking the necessary *remediation actions* on an ongoing basis to address identified weaknesses and deficiencies in the information system and its environment of operation?
- Does the organization have an effective process in place to report the *security status* of the information system and its environment of operation to the authorizing officials and other designated senior leaders within the organization on an ongoing basis?
- Is the organization updating critical *risk management documents* based on ongoing monitoring activities?
- Are authorizing officials conducting *ongoing security authorizations* by employing effective continuous monitoring activities and communicating updated risk determination and acceptance decisions to information system owners and common control providers?

FIGURE 5.18 NIST step 6 checkpoint.

Status

Periodically report the security status of the information system and control effectiveness to management during the operation/maintenance stage of the development life cycle.

Risk and Accept

Review the security status of the information system with management and determine if risk remains within acceptable tolerances or further plans of action are required during the operation/maintenance stage of the development life cycle.

Disposal

Implement a disposal strategy for when information systems are removed from service during the disposal stage of the development life cycle. The strategy should be designed to ensure appropriate sanitization of media and updating of asset inventories to support system decommission and/or disposal. When all tasks are completed, the system owner should be able to answer in the affirmative to the checkpoint questions in Figure 5.18.

Exception Handling

As part of any program, a process is required for handling exceptions to administrative, physical, and technical safeguards as a means of providing temporary relief. Exceptions should be formally documented, risk rated, tracked, and periodically reviewed. For example, in a situation where an administrative policy has been implemented requiring a password at least 10 characters in length, but an older system can only enforce 8 characters, a temporary exception might be warranted until an action plan can be completed to remediate the deficiency.

FIGURE 5.19 Measurement program structure.

Reporting and Metrics

Measurement and reporting of key risk indicators (KRIs) and key performance indicators (KPIs) is an important component to measuring program effectiveness.

As provided by NIST SP 800-55, an information security measurement program should include the four interdependent components shown in Figure 5.19.

The foundation is strong upper-level management support, for not only the success of the information security program but also the program's implementation. This support establishes a focus on information security within the highest levels of the organization. The second component is the existence of information security policies and procedures backed by the authority necessary to enforce compliance. Information security policies delineate the information security management structure, clearly assign information security responsibilities, and lay the foundation needed to reliably measure progress and compliance. Procedures document management's position on the implementation of an information security control and the rigor with which it is applied. Measures are not easily obtainable if no procedures are in place to supply data for measurement. The third component is developing and establishing quantifiable performance measures (e.g., KPIs, KRIs) that are designed to capture and provide meaningful performance data. To provide meaningful data, quantifiable information security measures must be based on information security performance goals and objectives, and be easily obtainable and feasible to measure. They must also be repeatable, provide relevant performance trends over time, and be useful for tracking performance and directing resources.

Finally, the information security measurement program itself must emphasize consistent periodic analysis of the measures data. Results of this analysis are used to apply lessons learned, improve effectiveness of existing security controls, and plan for the implementation of future security controls to meet new information security requirements as they occur. The success of an information security program implementation should be judged by the degree to which meaningful results are produced. A comprehensive information security measurement program should provide substantive justification for decisions that directly affect the information security posture of an organization.

KEY TERMS

Term	Definition
CIA	Confidentiality, integrity, and availability
PII	Personally identifiable information
PHI	Personal health information
NIST	National Institute of Standards and Technology
FIPS	Federal Information Processing Standards
ISO	International Organization for Standardization
Information governance	Structure (or framework) consisting of policies, processes, procedures, behaviors, and technologies designed to assist with managing information throughout its life cycle in a manner consistent with stakeholder expectations
Administrative safeguards	Actions, policies, and procedures involved in the selection, development, implementation, and maintenance of security measures
Physical safeguards	Physical measures to protect the organization's electronic information systems, data in physical form, buildings, and equipment from natural and environmental hazards and unauthorized intrusion
Technical safeguards	Technology and associated technical standards for its use to protect and control access to information
Head of agency	Highest-level official within an organization with overall responsibility for providing information security protections
Risk executive	Individual or group who ensures risk is viewed from an organization-wide perspective and risk is managed consistently
Chief Information Officer	Organizational official responsible for designating senior information security officer, maintaining policies and procedures, overseeing security personnel, and assisting and coordinating with senior officials regarding security matters
Information owner/steward	Organizational official with statutory, management, or operational authority for specified information and the responsibility for establishing the policies and procedures governing its generation, collection, processing, dissemination, and disposal
Senior information security officer	Also known as Chief Information Security Officer (CISO) or Chief Security Officer (CSO), is an organizational official responsible for carrying out security responsibilities and serving as primary liaison for Chief Information Officer

Term	Definition
Authorizing official	Senior official or executive with the authority to formally assume responsibility for operating an information system at an acceptable level of risk to organizational operations and assets, individuals, other organizations, and the Nation
Authorizing official designated representative	Organizational official who acts on behalf of an authorizing official to coordinate and conduct the required day-to-day activities associated with the security authorization process
Common control provider	Individual, group, or organization responsible for the development, implementation, assessment, and monitoring of common controls (i.e., security controls inherited by information systems)
Information system owner	Organizational official responsible for the procurement, development, integration, modification, operation, maintenance, and disposal of an information system
Information system security officer	Also known as information security officer (ISO), is an individual responsible for ensuring that the appropriate operational security posture is maintained for an information system and, as such, works in close collaboration with the information system owner
Information security architect	Individual, group, or organization responsible for ensuring that the information security requirements necessary to protect the organization's core missions and business processes are adequately addressed in all aspects of enterprise architecture including reference models, segment and solution architectures, and the resulting information systems supporting those missions and business processes
Information system security engineer	Individual, group, or organization responsible for conducting information system security engineering activities
Security control assessor	Individual, group, or organization responsible for conducting a comprehensive assessment of the management, operational, and technical security controls employed within or inherited by an information system to determine the overall effectiveness of the controls
Centralized governance	Authority, responsibility, and decision-making power are vested solely within central bodies
Decentralized governance	Authority, responsibility, and decision-making power are vested in and delegated to individual subordinate organizations within the parent organization
Hybrid governance	Authority, responsibility, and decision-making power are distributed between a central body and individual subordinate organizations
Framing	Understand the environment in which the organization operates and its risk tolerance (or appetite) to ensure risk is appropriately framed
Assessment	Identify threats, vulnerabilities, potential impact (harm) and likelihood harm will occur for the purpose of determining risk
Response	How an organization should respond to risk once identified

Term	Definition
Monitoring	Monitoring of risk over time for the purpose of evaluating control effectiveness, identifying system and environment changes that create risk, and ensuring risk responses are implemented in alignment with business objectives, regulatory requirements, and security and privacy policies, standards, and guidelines
Quantitative analysis	Analysis largely involving numbers (e.g., $10,000, $50,000, $100,000), visible properties, and statistics and a set of methods, principles, or rules for assessing risk
Qualitative analysis	Involves non-numerical categories or levels (e.g., low, moderate, high) and can be more effective when communicating with stakeholders. May also involve data such as themes, trends, or patterns of human behavior
Single loss expectancy (SLE)	Loss in monetary (e.g., dollars) terms associated with occurrence of a single event
Annual rate of occurrence (ARO)	Anticipated frequency that a single loss expectancy event is projected to occur in a 12-month period
Annual loss expectancy (ALE)	Expected loss over a 12-month period based on the single loss expectancy (SLE) of an event and the annual rate of occurrence (ARO)
Tangible loss	Involves direct (real) value of physical assets including revenue and server or facility costs
Intangible loss	Involves indirect value such as brand, reputation, and loss of prospective customers and intellectual property
Threat	Any event with the potential to adversely impact the confidentiality, integrity, or availability of information systems through unauthorized access, destruction, disclosure, or modification of information, or denial of service
Vulnerability	Sometimes referred to as exposure, any weakness in an information system such as servers, networks, and infrastructure that could be intentionally or unintentionally exploited by a threat
Controls	Sometimes referred to as safeguards, they are techniques, methods, policies, standards, processes, procedures, guidelines, and physical devices designed to reduce the vulnerability of an information asset or likelihood of successful vulnerability exploitation by a threat
Likelihood	Estimate of the likelihood (or probability) a threat will be motivated and capable of successfully exploiting a vulnerability
Impact	Expected harm or damage to an organization resulting from the successful exploitation of a vulnerability
Risk	Measure of the extent to which an organization is threatened by a particular event
Risk acceptance	Decision to accept a particular risk and its associated losses assuming it falls within an organization's risk tolerance

Term	Definition
Risk transfer	Decision to fully or partially transfer a particular risk and its associated losses to a third party such as vendor or insurance company
Risk mitigation	Decision to reduce vulnerabilities through implementation of additional administrative, physical, and/or technical safeguards
Risk avoidance	Decision to avoid taking actions or activities that would create new risk for the organization
Information risk management	Continuous life cycle beginning from the point information is created and ending when information is disposed, destroyed, or no longer requires protection
Information system development life cycle (SDLC)	Involves five phases including initiation (concept/requirements definition), development/acquisition, implementation, operation/maintenance, and disposal

Practice Exam

1. A structure consisting of policies, processes, procedures, behaviors, and technologies designed to assist with managing information throughout its life cycle is defined as:
   a. Administrative safeguards
   b. Privacy and security governance
   c. Physical safeguards
   d. Information governance

2. Actions, policies, and procedures involved in the selection, development, implementation, and maintenance of security measures are defined as:
   a. Administrative safeguards
   b. Privacy and security governance
   c. Physical safeguards
   d. Information governance

3. The Chief Information Officer is:
   a. The highest-level official within an organization with overall responsibility for providing information security protections
   b. Responsible for designating a senior information security officer
   c. Responsible for carrying out chief information security responsibilities
   d. An organizational official with statutory, management, or operational authority for specified information and the responsibility for establishing the policies and procedures governing its generation, collection, processing, dissemination, and disposal

4. The organizational official responsible for the procurement, development, integration, modification, operation, maintenance, and disposal of an information system is:

     a. Authorizing official

     b. Information owner/steward

     c. Information system owner

     d. Chief Information Officer

5. NIST SP 800-39 outlines approaches to information security governance that include all of the following except:

     a. Centralized

     b. Hybrid

     c. Decentralized

     d. Uniform

6. The International Organization for Standardization:

     a. Has published an information governance toolkit designed to enable organizations and partners to assess compliance with the various laws, policies, and standards associated with information governance

     b. Is responsible for the SP 800 series (computer security) and SP 500 series (information technology) publications relating to computer security

     c. Is responsible for publication of the 27002:2005 and 27799:2008 standards

     d. a and c

7. Framing involves:

     a. Understanding the environment in which the organization operates

     b. Understanding risk tolerance to ensure risk is appropriately framed

     c. Assessing risk to identify threats, vulnerabilities, potential impact, and likelihood of harm

     d. Evaluating risk over time for the purpose of evaluating control effectiveness, identifying system and environment changes that create risk, and ensuring risk responses are implemented in alignment with business objectives, regulatory requirements, and security and privacy policies, standards, and guidelines

8. Qualitative assessments:

     a. Involve non-numerical categories or levels (e.g., low, moderate, high) and can be more effective when communicating with stakeholders

     b. Involve an analysis largely involving numbers (e.g., $10,000, $50,000, $100,000), visible properties, and statistics and a set of methods, principles, or rules for assessing risk

     c. a and b

     d. None of the above

9. Annual loss expectancy (ALE) is:

     a. The anticipated frequency that a single loss expectancy (SLE) event is projected to occur in a 12-month period

     b. The expected loss over a 12-month period based on the SLE of an event and the annual rate of occurrence (ARO)

     c. $ALE = SLE \times ARO$

     d. b and c

10. A vulnerability is:
    a. Any event with the potential to adversely impact the confidentiality, integrity, or availability of information systems through unauthorized access, destruction, disclosure, or modification of information, or denial of service
    b. Any weakness in an information system such as servers, networks, and infrastructure that could be intentionally or unintentionally exploited by a threat
    c. A measure of the extent to which an organization is threatened by a particular event
    d. a and c

11. A risk is:
    a. Any event with the potential to adversely impact the confidentiality, integrity, or availability of information systems through unauthorized access, destruction, disclosure, or modification of information, or denial of service
    b. Any weakness in an information system such as servers, networks, and infrastructure that could be intentionally or unintentionally exploited by a threat
    c. A measure of the extent to which an organization is threatened by a particular event
    d. a and c

12. Risk treatment generally involves the following options:
    a. Transfer, acceptance, mitigate, eliminate
    b. Acceptance, transmit, mitigate, deflect
    c. Avoid, transfer, eliminate, manage
    d. Mitigate, transfer, acceptance, avoid

13. Which one of the following formulas is incorrect?
    a. Managed risk = residual risk − inherent risk
    b. SLE = asset value × exposure
    c. ALE = SLE − ARO
    d. a and c

14. Controls are:
    a. Any weakness in an information system such as servers, networks, and infrastructure that could be intentionally or unintentionally exploited by a threat
    b. Techniques, methods, policies, standards, processes, procedures, guidelines, and physical devices designed to increase the vulnerability of an information asset
    c. Techniques, methods, policies, standards, processes, procedures, guidelines, and physical devices designed to decrease the vulnerability of an information asset
    d. Techniques, methods, policies, standards, processes, procedures, guidelines, and physical devices designed to maintain the vulnerability of an information asset

15. Likelihood is:
    a. The expected harm or damage to an organization resulting from the successful exploitation of a vulnerability
    b. The probability a vulnerability will be motivated and capable of exploiting a threat
    c. A measure of the extent to which an organization is threatened by a particular event
    d. None of the above
16. The categorization of information systems, selection, implementation, and assessment of security controls, authorization of information systems, and monitoring of security controls are steps included in the:
    a. Information governance process
    b. System development life cycle
    c. IT governance process
    d. Information risk management life cycle
17. Intangible loss involves:
    a. Direct (real) value of physical assets including revenue and server or facility costs
    b. Indirect value such as brand, reputation, and loss of prospective customers and intellectual property
    c. Indirect value such as revenue and server or facility costs
    d. None of the above
18. The information system development life cycle includes the following phases:
    a. Initiation, development/acquisition, monitoring, disposal
    b. Disposal, initiation, operational/maintenance, development/acquisition
    c. Categorization, selection, implementation, authorization, monitoring
    d. Selection, implementation, monitoring, disposal
19. Centralized governance is defined as:
    a. Authority, responsibility, and decision-making powers that are distributed between a central body and individual subordinate organizations
    b. Structure (or framework) consisting of policies, processes, procedures, behaviors, and technologies designed to assist with managing information throughout its life cycle in a manner consistent with stakeholder expectations
    c. Authority, responsibility, and decision-making powers that are vested solely within central bodies
    d. Authority, responsibility, and decision-making powers that are vested in and delegated to individual subordinate organizations within the parent organization
20. Risk transfer involves:
    a. A decision to avoid taking actions or activities that would create new risk for the organization

b. Decision to accept a particular risk and its associated losses assuming it falls within an organization's risk tolerance

c. Decision to reduce vulnerabilities through implementation of additional administrative, physical, and/or technical safeguards

d. None of the above

Practice Exam Answers

1. d
2. a
3. b
4. c
5. d
6. c
7. a
8. a
9. d
10. b
11. c
12. d
13. d
14. c
15. d
16. d
17. b
18. b
19. c
20. d

References

National Health Service, n.d. Information Governance Toolkit. IG Toolkit Home. Web. June 29, 2014. <https://www.igt.hscic.gov.uk/Home.aspx?tk(414078609082725&cb(3d2de24d-bef5-4339-b5d2-f6cdb29e6a21&lnv(7&clnav(YES>.

National Institute of Standards and Technology, n.d. Guide for Conducting Risk Assessments. NIST Computer Security Publications – NIST Special Publications (SPs). Version SP 800-30 rev1. Web. June 29, 2014. <http://csrc.nist.gov/publications/nistpubs/800-30-rev1/sp800_30_r1.pdf>.

U.S. Department of Health & Human Services, n.d. 45 CFR Parts 160, 162, and 164 Health Insurance Reform: Security Standards; Final Rule. Health Information Privacy. Web. June 29, 2014. <http://www.hhs.gov/ocr/privacy/hipaa/administrative/securityrule/securityrulepdf.pdf>.

U.S. Department of Health & Human Services, n.d. Guidance on Risk Analysis Requirements Under the HIPAA Security Rule. Health Information Privacy. Web. June 29, 2014. <http://www.hhs.gov/ocr/privacy/hipaa/administrative/securityrule/rafinalguidancepdf.pdf>.

International Organization for Standardization, n.d. Home. About ISO. Web. June 28, 2014. <http://www.iso.org/iso/home/about.htm>.

International Organization for Standardization, n.d. Home. ISO/IEC 27002:2005. Web. June 29, 2014. <http://www.iso.org/iso/catalogue_detail?csnumber(50297>.

National Institute of Standards and Technology, n.d. Search. NIST Computer Security Publications. Web. June 27, 2014. <http://csrc.nist.gov/publications/PubsSPs.html>.

National Institute of Standards and Technology, n.d. About NIST. Web. June 29, 2014. <http://www.nist.gov/public_affairs/nandyou.cfm>.

National Institute of Standards and Technology, n.d. Hot Topics. NIST Computer Security Division. Web. June 29, 2014. <http://csrc.nist.gov>.

National Institute of Standards and Technology, n.d. Guide for Applying the Risk Management Framework to Federal Information Systems. Computer Security Division, Computer Security Resource Center. Version SP 800-37 rev1. Web. June 29, 2014. <http://csrc.nist.gov/publications/nistpubs/800-37-rev1/sp800-37-rev1-final.pdf>.

Centers for Medicare & Medicaid Services, n.d. CMS Information Security Risk Assessment (IS RA) Procedure. CMS Information Security Overview. Centers for Medicare & Medicaid Services. Version 1.0. Web. June 29, 2014. <https://www.cms.gov/Research-Statistics-Data-and-Systems/CMS-Information-Technology/InformationSecurity/downloads/IS_RA_Procedure.pdf>.

International Organization for Standardization, n.d. Home. ISO 27799:2008. Web. June 29, 2014. <http://www.iso.org/iso/catalogue_detail?csnumber(41298>.

National Institute of Standards and Technology, n.d. Managing Information Security Risk: Organization, Mission, and Information System View. Computer Security Division, Computer Security Resource Center. Version SP 800-39. Web. June 29, 2014. <http://csrc.nist.gov/publications/nistpubs/800-39/SP800-39-final.pdf>.

National Institute of Standards and Technology, n.d. Performance Measurement Guide for Information Security. Computer Security Division, Computer Security Resource Center. Version SP 800-55 rev1. Web. June 29, 2014. <http://csrc.nist.gov/publications/nistpubs/800-55-Rev1/SP800-55-rev1.pdf>.

Information Risk Assessment

- Understand risk assessment
- Identify and use assessment control procedures
- Understand the risk assessment process
- Understand the risk response and remediation process

INTRODUCTION

Healthcare organizations have an increasing reliance on information technology and information systems to carry out their mission. These technologies and systems are subject to serious threats that can have an adverse impact on the confidentiality, integrity, and availability of organizational operations and assets. As a result, it is important that organizations implement risk assessment processes as part of an overall governance program to assist with continuously monitoring the effectiveness of administrative, physical, and technical safeguards.

Knowledge Areas

After reviewing this chapter and supporting reference materials, HCISPP candidates should comprehend the importance and purpose of conducting information risk assessments. This includes identifying assessment control procedures, the process for conducting a risk assessment, and the process to respond and remediate risk.

UNDERSTANDING RISK ASSESSMENT

Risk assessments are a core component of any information risk management program, can be qualitative and/or quantitative in nature, and are designed to identify, estimate, and prioritize risk associated with the operation and use of information systems.

131

Key Terms
Let us briefly review key terms associated with information risk assessment:

- **Risk**: Measure of the extent to which an organization is threatened by a particular event.
- **Information life cycle**: Continuous life cycle beginning from the point information is created and ending when information is disposed or destroyed.
- **Threat**: Any event with the potential to adversely impact the confidentiality, integrity, or availability of information systems through unauthorized access, destruction, disclosure, or modification of information, or denial of service.
- **Vulnerability**: Sometimes referred to as exposure, any weakness in an information system such as servers, networks, and infrastructure that could be intentionally or unintentionally exploited by a threat.
- **Controls**: Sometimes referred to as safeguards, they are techniques, methods, policies, standards, processes, procedures, guidelines, and physical devices designed to reduce the vulnerability of an information asset or likelihood of successful vulnerability exploitation by a threat.
- **Likelihood**: Estimate of the likelihood (or probability) a threat will be motivated and capable of exploiting a vulnerability.
- **Impact**: Expected harm or damage to an organization resulting from the successful exploitation of a vulnerability.
- **Risk acceptance**: Decision to accept a particular risk and its associated losses assuming it falls within an organization's risk tolerance.
- **Risk transfer**: Decision to fully or partially transfer a particular risk and its associated losses to a third party such as vendor or insurance company.
- **Risk mitigation**: Decision to reduce vulnerabilities through implementation of additional administrative, physical, and/or technical safeguards.
- **Risk avoidance**: Decision to avoid taking actions or activities that would create new risk for the organization.

Life Cycle and Continuous Monitoring
As discussed in Chapter 5, the information life cycle begins when information is first created and continues until such time as the information is disposed of or destroyed. As a result, risk assessments cannot be simply one-time activities with the hope of providing long-term and definitive information, but must be performed periodically throughout the information life cycle to:

- Protect the confidentiality, integrity, and availability of information; and
- Guide and inform decision makers in their response to risks.

In addition to periodic risk assessments, information and systems should be continuously monitored to ensure control effectiveness and identify potential threats, events, or changes warranting risk analysis.

Tools, Resources, and Techniques

While various tools, resources, and techniques exist to assist healthcare organizations with the performance and maintenance of information risk assessments, all share similar principles and objectives. However, selection will vary based on a number of factors including, but not limited to, cost and an organization's requirements, culture, and size.

NIST Guide for Conducting Risk Assessments

NIST's Special Publication 800-30 provides guidance for conducting risk assessments of federal information systems and organizations. It is intended to serve a diverse group of risk management professionals including:

- Individuals with oversight responsibilities for risk management (e.g., heads of agencies, chief executive officers, chief operating officers, risk executives);
- Individuals with responsibilities for conducting organizational missions/business functions (e.g., mission/business owners, information owners/stewards, authorizing officials);
- Individuals with responsibilities for acquiring information technology products, services, or information systems (e.g., acquisition officials, procurement officers, contracting officers);
- Individuals with information system/security design, development, and implementation responsibilities (e.g., program managers, enterprise architects, information security architects, information system/security engineers, information systems integrators);
- Individuals with information security oversight, management, and operational responsibilities (e.g., chief information officers, senior information security officers, information security managers, information system owners, common control providers); and
- Individuals with information security/risk assessment and monitoring responsibilities (e.g., system evaluators, penetration testers, security control assessors, risk assessors, independent verifiers/validators, inspectors general, auditors).

ISO/IEC 27005:2011

The ISO/IEC 27005:2011 standard provides guidance for information security risk management including the performance of risk assessments. As described by ISO, "it supports the general concepts specified in ISO/IEC 27001 and is designed to assist the satisfactory implementation of information security based on a risk management approach."

Desired Outcomes

The purpose of a risk assessment in terms of the information it is intended to produce and the decisions it is intended to support must be defined to achieve a desired outcome. Their intent is to inform decision makers and support risk responses by identifying:

■ Relevant threats to an organization;
■ Internal and external vulnerabilities;
■ Potential impact resulting from a threat exploiting a vulnerability; and
■ Likelihood that impact will occur or be realized.

Role of Internal and External Audit

Internal and external audit provide organizations with an independent perspective regarding information security program and control effectiveness in protecting the confidentiality, integrity, and availability of information. While internal audit departments typically review various security controls on a periodic basis, organizations should understand the Health Information Technology for Economic and Clinical Health Act (HITECH) also requires Health and Human Services (HHS) to perform periodic external audits of covered entity and business associate compliance with HIPAA Privacy, Security, and Breach Notification Rules.

ASSESSMENT PROCEDURES

As defined by NIST Special Publication 800-53A Revision 1, an assessment procedure consists of a set of assessment objectives, each with an associated set of potential assessment methods and assessment objects.

Assessment Objective

An assessment objective includes a set of determination statements related to the security control under assessment. The determination statements are linked to the content of the security control (i.e., the security control functionality) to ensure traceability of assessment results back to the fundamental control requirements. The application of an assessment procedure to a security control produces assessment findings. These assessment findings reflect, or are subsequently used, to help determine the overall effectiveness of the security control.

Assessment Object

Assessment objects identify the specific items being assessed and include specifications, mechanisms, activities, and individuals:

■ Specifications are the document-based artifacts (e.g., policies, procedures, plans, system security requirements, functional specifications, and architectural designs) associated with an information system.
■ Mechanisms are the specific hardware, software, or firmware safeguards and countermeasures employed within an information system.
■ Activities are the specific protection-related pursuits or actions supporting an information system that involve people (e.g., conducting system backup operations, monitoring network traffic, exercising a contingency plan).

- Individuals, or groups of individuals, are people applying the specifications, mechanisms, or activities described earlier.

Assessment Methods

Assessment methods define the nature of the assessor actions and include:

Examine method: The process of reviewing, inspecting, observing, studying, or analyzing one or more assessment objects (i.e., specifications, mechanisms, or activities). The purpose of the examine method is to facilitate assessor understanding, achieve clarification, or obtain evidence.

Interview method: The process of holding discussions with individuals or groups of individuals within an organization to, once again, facilitate assessor understanding, achieve clarification, or obtain evidence.

Test method: The process of exercising one or more assessment objects (i.e., activities or mechanisms) under specified conditions to compare actual with expected behavior.

In all three methods, the results are used in making specific determinations called for in the determination statements and thereby achieving the objectives for the assessment procedure.

NIST Example

The first assessment objective for CP-2 is derived from the basic control statement (Figure 6.1). Potential assessment methods and objects are added to the assessment procedure (Figure 6.2).

SECURITY CONTROL	
CP-2	**CONTINGENCY PLAN**

Control:	The organization:
	a. Develops a contingency plan for the information system that:
	  - Identifies essential missions and business functions and associated contingency requirements;
	  - Provides recovery objectives, restoration priorities, and metrics;
	  - Addresses contingency roles, responsibilities, assigned individuals with contact information;
	  - Addresses maintaining essential missions and business functions despite an information system disruption, compromise, or failure;
	  - Addresses eventual, full information system restoration without deterioration of the security measures originally planned and implemented; and
	  - Is reviewed and approved by designated officials within the organization;
	b. Distributes copies of the contingency plan to [*Assignment: organization-defined list of key contingency personnel (identified by name and/or by role) and organizational elements*];
	c. Coordinates contingency planning activities with incident handling activities;
	d. Reviews the contingency plan for the information system [*Assignment: organization-defined frequency*];
	e. Revises the contingency plan to address changes to the organization, information system, or environment of operation and problems encountered during contingency plan implementation, execution, or testing; and
	f. Communicates contingency plan changes to [*Assignment: organization-defined list of key contingency personnel (identified by name and/or by role) and organizational elements*].

FIGURE 6.1 NIST example contingency plan security control.

ASSESSMENT PROCEDURE	

CP-2.1	**ASSESSMENT OBJECTIVE:**
	Determine if:
	(i) the organization develops a contingency plan for the information system that:
	   - identifies essential missions and business functions and associated contingency requirements;
	   - provides recovery objectives, restoration priorities, and metrics;
	   - addresses contingency roles, responsibilities, assigned individuals with contact information;
	   - addresses maintaining essential missions and business functions despite an information system disruption, compromise, or failure; and
	   - addresses eventual, full information system restoration without deterioration of the security measures originally planned and implemented; and
	   - is reviewed and approved by designated officials within the organization;
	(ii) the organization defines key contingency personnel (identified by name and/or by role) and organizational elements designated to receive copies of the contingency plan; and
	(iii) the organization distributes copies of the contingency plan to organization-defined key contingency personnel and organizational elements.
	
	POTENTIAL ASSESSMENT METHODS AND OBJECTS:
	Examine: [*SELECT FROM:* Contingency planning policy; procedures addressing contingency operations for the information system; contingency plan; security plan; other relevant documents or records].[25]
	Interview: [*SELECT FROM:* Organizational personnel with contingency planning and plan implementation responsibilities].

FIGURE 6.2 NIST example assessment procedure.

In a similar manner, the second assessment objective and potential assessment methods and objects for CP-2 are established (Figure 6.3).

ASSESSMENT PROCEDURE	
CP-2.2	*Determine if:* (i) the organization coordinates contingency planning activities with incident handling activities; (ii) the organization defines the frequency of contingency plan reviews; (iii) the organization reviews the contingency plan for the information system in accordance with the organization-defined frequency; (iv) the organization revises the contingency plan to address changes to the organization, information system, or environment of operation and problems encountered during contingency plan implementation, execution, or testing; and (v) the organization communicates contingency plan changes to the key contingency personnel and organizational elements as identified in CP-2.1 (ii). **POTENTIAL ASSESSMENT METHODS AND OBJECTS:** **Examine:** [*SELECT FROM:* Contingency planning policy; procedures addressing contingency operations for the information system; contingency plan; security plan; other relevant documents or records]. **Interview:** [*SELECT FROM:* Organizational personnel with contingency planning and plan implementation responsibilities; organizational personnel with incident handling responsibilities].

FIGURE 6.3 NIST example assessment procedure (continued).

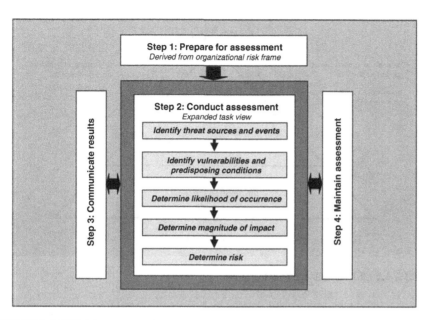

FIGURE 6.4 NIST risk assessment process.

RISK ASSESSMENT PROCESS

In Chapter 5 we reviewed roles and responsibilities and four key components associated with a holistic risk management process that include risk framing, assessment, response, and monitoring as outlined by NIST SP 800-30. This section focuses on the assessment component and the four-step process of assessing information security risk:

- Prepare for the assessment.
- Conduct the assessment.
- Communicate assessment results.
- Maintain the assessment.

Figure 6.4 illustrates the relationship between these steps and their supporting set of tasks discussed later in this chapter.

Risk Assessment Hierarchy

Risk assessments can be conducted at all three tiers in the risk management hierarchy:

- Tier 1 (organization level);
- Tier 2 (mission/business process level); and
- Tier 3 (information system level).

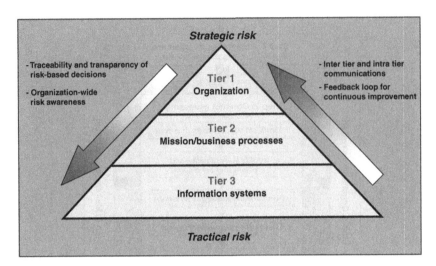

FIGURE 6.5 NIST risk management hierarchy.

At Tiers 1 and 2, organizations use risk assessments to evaluate areas such as systemic information security-related risks associated with organizational governance and management activities, mission/business processes, enterprise architecture, or funding of information security programs. At Tier 3, organizations use risk assessments to more effectively support implementation of the information risk management life cycle processes and activities described in Chapter 5. Figure 6.5 illustrates the risk management hierarchy defined in NIST SP 800-39, which provides multiple risk perspectives from a strategic to tactical level. Traditional risk assessments have generally focused on Tier 3, which can result in overlooking other significant risk factors more appropriately assessed at Tiers 1 or 2. Risk assessments also support risk response decisions at different tiers of the risk management hierarchy.

Tier 1: Organizational Level

At Tier 1, risk assessments support organizational strategies, policies, guidance, and processes for managing risk. Risk assessments conducted at Tier 1 focus on organizational operations, assets, and individuals – comprehensive assessments across mission/business lines. For example, Tier 1 risk assessments may address:

- The specific types of threats directed at an organization and how those threats affect policy decisions;
- Systemic weaknesses or deficiencies discovered in multiple organizational information systems capable of being exploited by threats;
- The potential adverse impact on organizations from the loss or compromise of organizational information (either intentionally or unintentionally); and

- The use of new information and computing technologies such as mobile and cloud and the potential effect on the ability of organizations to successfully carry out their missions/business operations while using those technologies.

Tier 1 risk assessments can also affect:

- Organization-wide information security programs, policies, procedures, and guidance;
- Risk management organizational structure;
- The types of appropriate risk responses or treatments;
- Investment and procurement decisions for information technologies/ systems;
- Minimum organization-wide security controls;
- Conformance to enterprise/security architectures; and
- Monitoring strategies and ongoing authorizations of information systems and common controls.

Tier 2: Mission/Business Process

At Tier 2, risk assessments support the determination of mission/business process protection and resiliency requirements. They also support the allocation of these requirements to enterprise architecture. This allocation is accomplished through an information security architecture embedded within the enterprise architecture. Tier 2 risk assessments also inform and guide decisions on whether, how, and when to use information systems for specific mission/business processes, in particular for alternative mission/business processing in the face of compromised information systems. Tier 2 risk assessments can also affect:

- Enterprise architecture/security architecture design decisions;
- The selection of common controls and suppliers, services, and contractors to support organizational missions/business functions;
- The development of risk-aware mission/business processes; and
- The interpretation of information security policies with respect to organizational information systems and environments in which those systems operate.

Tier 3: Information System

The Tier 2 context and the system development life cycle determine the purpose and define the scope of risk assessment activities at Tier 3. While initial risk assessments (those performed for the first time vs. updating prior risk assessments) can be performed at any phase in the system development life cycle, they should be performed ideally during the initiation phase. In the initiation phase, risk assessments evaluate the anticipated vulnerabilities and presumed conditions affecting the confidentiality, integrity, and availability of information systems in the context of the planned operational environment. Such assessments inform risk response, enabling information system owners/ program managers and mission/business owners to make the final decisions about the necessary security controls based on the security categorization and environment of operation. Risk assessments are also conducted at later phases in the system development life cycle and update risk assessment results from earlier phases. These risk assessment results for as-built or as-deployed information systems typically include descriptions of vulnerabilities in the systems, an assessment of the risks associated with each vulnerability (thereby updating the assessment of vulnerability severity), and corrective actions that can be taken to mitigate the risks. Tier 3 risk assessments can also affect:

- Design decisions (including the selection, tailoring, and supplementation of security controls and the selection of information technology products for organizational information systems);
- Implementation decisions (including whether specific information technology products or product configurations meet security control requirements); and
- Operational decisions (including the requisite level of monitoring activity, the frequency of ongoing information system authorizations, system maintenance decisions, and possibly addition of controls to address coverage gaps).

Step 1: Prepare

The first step in the process is assessment preparation and involves five supporting tasks:

- Identify purpose.
- Identify scope.
- Identify assumptions and constraints.
- Identify information sources.
- Identify risk model and analytic approach.

Task 1-1: Identify Purpose

Identify the purpose of the risk assessment in terms of the information that the assessment is intended to produce and the decisions the assessment is intended to support. The purpose should be explicitly stated in sufficient detail to ensure the assessment produces the appropriate information and supports the intended decisions. Each organization can determine how best to capture and present information produced during the risk assessment.

At Tier 1, risk assessments:

- Support the risk executive (function); and
- Serve as a key input to the risk management strategy.

At Tier 2, risk assessments enable organizations to:

- Understand dependencies and ways in which risks are treated among information systems that support organizational mission/business processes;
- Support architectural and operational decisions for organizational risk responses;
- Identify trends to enable proactive risk response strategies and courses of action for mission/business processes to be defined; and
- Support reciprocity, particularly to enable information sharing.

At Tier 3, risk assessments support:

- Authorization-related decisions throughout the system development life cycle;
- Reciprocity, particularly for reuse of assessment information;
- Risk management activities at Tier 2; and
- Programmatic risk management activities throughout the system development life cycle.

Risk assessments can also have a very specific purpose such as answering a question (e.g., What are the risk implications of a newly discovered vulnerability or class of vulnerabilities, allowing new connectivity, outsourcing a specific function, or adopting a new technology?). The purpose of a risk assessment is influenced by whether it is an initial assessment (first time) or a subsequent assessment initiated from the risk response or monitoring steps in the risk management process.

For initial assessments, the purpose can include:

- Establishing a baseline assessment of risk; or
- Identifying threats and vulnerabilities, impacts to organizational operations and assets, individuals, and other organizations, and other risk factors to be tracked over time as part of risk monitoring.

For reassessments, the purpose can include:

- Providing a comparative analysis of alternative risk responses or answering a specific question;
- Updating the risk assessment based on:
  - Ongoing determinations of the effectiveness of security controls in organizational information systems or operational environments;
  - Changes to information systems or operational environments (e.g., changes to hardware, firmware, software; changes to system-specific, hybrid, or common controls; changes to mission/business processes, common infrastructure and support services, threats, vulnerabilities, or facilities); and
  - Results from compliance verification activities.

Reassessments may also be initiated by organizations due to incidents that have occurred (e.g., cyber attacks compromising organizational information or information systems).

Task 1-2: Identify Scope

Identify the scope of the risk assessment in terms of organizational applicability, time frame supported, and architectural/technology considerations. The scope determines what will be considered in the assessment, affects the range of information available to make risk-based decisions, and is determined by the organizational official requesting the assessment and the risk management strategy. Establishing the scope of the risk assessment helps organizations to determine:

- What tiers are addressed in the assessment;
- What parts of organizations are affected by the assessment and how they are affected;
- What decisions the assessment results support;
- How long assessment results are relevant; and
- What influences the need to update the assessment.

Establishing the scope of the risk assessment also helps to determine the form and content of the risk assessment report, as well as the information to be shared as a result of conducting the assessment. At Tier 3, the scope of a risk assessment can depend on the authorization boundary for the information system.

Organizational Applicability

Organizational applicability describes which parts of the organization or sub-organizations are affected by the risk assessment and resulting risk-based decisions. For example, the risk assessment can inform decisions regarding information systems supporting a particular organizational mission/business function or process. This can include decisions regarding the selection, tailoring, or supplementation of security controls for specific information systems or the selection of common controls. Alternatively, the risk assessment can inform decisions regarding a set of closely related missions/business functions or processes. The scope of the risk assessment may include not only the missions/business functions, mission/business processes, common infrastructure, or shared services on which the organization currently depends but also those which the organization might use under specific operational conditions.

Effectiveness Time Frame

Organizations determine how long the results of particular risk assessments can be used to legitimately inform risk-based decisions, which is usually related to assessment purpose. For example, a risk assessment to inform Tier 1 policy-related decisions needs to be relevant for an extended period of time since the governance process for policy changes can be time-consuming in many organizations. On the other hand, a risk assessment conducted to inform a Tier 3 decision regarding the use of a compensating security control for an information system may be relevant only until the next release of the information technology product providing the required security capability. Organizations determine the useful life of risk assessment results and under what conditions the current assessment results become ineffective or irrelevant. Risk monitoring can also be used to help determine the effectiveness of time frames for risk assessments and the need to refresh existing controls to address a changing threat landscape.

Architectural/Technology Considerations

Organizations use architectural and technology considerations to clarify the scope of the risk assessment. At Tier 2, for example, the scope of the risk assessment can be defined in terms of the mission/business segment architecture (e.g., including all systems, services, and infrastructures that support a specific mission/function). For a targeted risk assessment at any tier, the specific question to be answered can restrict the scope to a specific technology. At Tier 3, for example, the scope of the risk assessment can be an organizational information system in its operational environment. This entails placing the information system in its architectural context, so that vulnerabilities within inherited controls can be taken into consideration. Alternately, the scope of the assessment can be limited solely to the information system, without consideration of inherited vulnerabilities.

Task 1-3: Identify Assumptions and Constraints

Identify the specific assumptions and constraints under which the risk assessment is conducted. As part of the risk framing step in the risk management process, organizations make explicit the specific assumptions, constraints, risk tolerance, and priorities/trade-offs used within organizations to make investment and operational decisions, which guides and informs organizational risk assessments. When an organizational risk management strategy cannot be cited, risk assessments identify and document assumptions and constraints. Assumptions and constraints identified by organizations during the risk framing step and included as part of the organizational risk management strategy need not be repeated in each individual risk assessment. By making assumptions and constraints explicit, there is greater clarity in the risk model selected for the risk assessment, increased reproducibility/repeatability of assessment results, and an increased opportunity for reciprocity among organizations. Organizations identify assumptions in key areas relevant to the risk assessment including, for example:

- Threat sources and events;
- Vulnerabilities and predisposing conditions;

- Potential impacts;
- Assessment and analysis approaches; and
- Which missions/business functions are primary.

Organizations also identify constraints in key areas relevant to the risk assessment including, for example:

- Resources available for the assessment;
- Skills and expertise required for the assessment; and
- Operational considerations related to mission/business activities.

Finally, organizations consider the uncertainty with regard to assumptions made or other information used in the risk assessment, as uncertainty can affect organizational risk tolerance. For example, assumptions based on a lack of specific or credible information may reduce an organization's risk tolerance because of the uncertainty influencing the assumptions. The following are examples of areas where assumptions/constraints for risk assessments may be identified.

Threat Sources

Organizations need to determine which types of threat sources are to be considered during risk assessments. Organizations make explicit the process used to identify threats and any assumptions related to the threat identification process. If such information is identified during the risk framing step and included as part of the organizational risk management strategy, the information need not be repeated in each individual risk assessment. Risk assessments can address all types of threat sources, a single broad threat source (e.g., adversarial) or a specific threat source (e.g., trusted insider).

Threat Events

Organizations need to determine which type of threat events are to be considered during risk assessments and the level of detail needed to describe such events. Descriptions of threat events can be expressed in highly general terms (e.g., phishing, distributed denial-of-service), in more descriptive terms using tactics, techniques, and procedures, or in highly specific terms (e.g., the names of specific information systems, technologies, organizations, roles, or locations). In addition, organizations consider what representative set of threat events can serve as a starting point for the identification of the specific threat events in the risk assessment and what degree of confirmation is needed for threat events to be considered relevant for purposes of the risk assessment. For example, organizations may consider only those threat events that have been observed (either internally or by organizations that are peers/partners) or all probable threat events.

Vulnerabilities and Predisposing Conditions

Organizations need to determine the types of vulnerabilities that are to be considered during risk assessments and the level of detail provided in the vulnerability descriptions. Organizations make explicit the process used to identify vulnerabilities and any assumptions related to the vulnerability identification process. If such information is identified during the risk framing step and included as part of the organizational risk management strategy, the information need not be repeated in each individual risk assessment. Vulnerabilities can be associated with organizational information systems (e.g., hardware, software, firmware, internal controls, and security procedures) or the environments in which those systems operate (e.g., organizational governance, external relationships, mission/business processes, enterprise architectures, information security architectures). Organizations also determine the types of conditions that are to be considered during risk assessments including, for example, architectures and technologies employed, operational environments, and personnel.

Likelihood
Organizations need to make explicit the process used to conduct likelihood determinations and any assumptions related to the likelihood determination process. If such information is identified during the risk framing step and included as part of the organizational risk management strategy, the information need not be repeated in each individual risk assessment.

Impacts
Organizations need to determine potential adverse impacts in terms of organizational operations (i.e., missions, functions, image, and reputation), organizational assets, individuals, and other organizations. Organizations make explicit the process used to conduct impact determinations and any assumptions related to the impact determination process. If such information is identified during the risk framing step and included as part of the organizational risk management strategy, the information need not be repeated in each individual risk assessment. Organizations address impacts at a level of detail that includes, for example, specific mission/business processes or information resources (e.g., information, personnel, equipment, funds, and information technology). Organizations may include information from an impact analysis with regard to providing impact information for risk assessments.

Risk Tolerance and Uncertainty
Organizations need to determine the levels and types of risk that are acceptable. Risk tolerance is determined as part of the organizational risk management strategy to ensure consistency across the organization. Organizations also provide guidance on how to identify reasons for uncertainty when risk factors are assessed, since uncertainty in one or more factors will propagate to the resulting evaluation of level of risk, and how to compensate for incomplete, imperfect, or assumption-dependent estimates. Consideration of uncertainty is

especially important when organizations consider advanced persistent threats (APTs) since assessments of the likelihood of threat event occurrence can have a great degree of uncertainty. To compensate, organizations can take a variety of approaches to determine likelihood, ranging from assuming the worst-case likelihood (certain to happen sometime in the foreseeable future) to assuming that if an event has not been observed, it is unlikely to happen. In determining likelihood, they should also consider the probability of an attack being attempted and its probability of success. Organizations also determine what levels of risk (combination of likelihood and impact) indicate that no further analysis of any risk factors is needed.

Analytic Approach

Risk assessments include both assessment approaches (i.e., quantitative, qualitative) and analysis approaches (i.e., threat-oriented, asset/impact-oriented, vulnerability-oriented). Together, the assessment and analysis approaches form the analytic approach for the risk assessment. Organizations determine the level of detail and the form in which threats are analyzed including the level of granularity to describe threat events or threat scenarios. Different analysis approaches can lead to different levels of detail in characterizing adverse events for which likelihoods are determined. For example, an adverse event could be characterized in several ways (with increasing levels of detail):

- A threat event (for which the likelihood is determined by taking the maximum overall threat sources);
- A pairing of a threat event and a threat source; or
- A detailed threat scenario/attack tree.

In general, organizations can be expected to require more detail for highly critical missions/business functions, common infrastructures, or shared services on which multiple missions or business functions depend (as common points of failure), and information systems with high criticality or sensitivity. Mission/business owners may also amplify this guidance for risk hot spots (e.g., information systems, services, or critical infrastructure components of particular concern) in mission/business segments.

Task 1-4: Identify Information Sources

Identify the sources of descriptive, threat, vulnerability, and impact information to be used in the risk assessment. Descriptive information enables organizations to be able to determine the relevance of threat and vulnerability information.

At Tier 1, descriptive information can include:

- The type of risk management and information security governance structures in place within organizations; and

- How the organization identifies and prioritizes critical missions/ business functions.

At Tier 2, descriptive information can include information about:

- Organizational mission/business processes, functional management processes, and information flows;
- Enterprise architecture, information security architecture, and the technical/process flow architectures of the systems, common infrastructures, and shared services that fall within the scope of the risk assessment; and
- The external environments in which organizations operate including the relationships and dependencies with external providers.

Such information is typically found in architectural documentation (particularly documentation of high-level operational views), business continuity plans, and risk assessment reports for organizational information systems, common infrastructures, and shared services that fall within the scope of the risk assessment.

At Tier 3, descriptive information can include information about:

- The design of and technologies used in organizational information systems;
- The environment in which the systems operate;
- Connectivity to and dependency on other information systems; and
- Dependencies on common infrastructures or shared services.

Such information is found in system documentation, contingency plans, and risk assessment reports for other information systems, infrastructures, and services. Sources of information can be either internal or external to organizations. Internal sources of information that can provide insights into both threats and vulnerabilities can include risk assessment reports, incident reports, security logs, trouble tickets, and monitoring results. Note that internally, information from risk assessment reports at one tier can serve as input to risk assessments at other tiers. Mission/business owners are encouraged to identify not only common infrastructure and/or support services they depend on but also those they might use under specific operational circumstances. External sources of threat information can include cross-community organizations [e.g., US Computer Emergency Readiness Team (US-CERT), Information Sharing and Analysis Centers (ISACs) for critical infrastructure sectors], research and nongovernmental organizations (e.g., Carnegie Mellon University, Software Engineering Institute – CERT), and security service providers. Organizations using external sources should consider the timeliness, specificity, and relevance of threat information. Similar to sources of threat information, sources of vulnerability information can also be either internal or external to organizations. Information about predisposing conditions can be found in a variety of sources including descriptions of information systems, operational environments, shared services, common infrastructures, and enterprise architecture. Sources of impact information can include mission/business impact analyses, information system component inventories, and security categorizations. Security categorization constitutes a determination of the potential impacts should certain events occur that jeopardize the information and information systems needed by the organization to accomplish its assigned missions, protect its assets, fulfill its legal responsibilities, maintain its day-to-day functions, and protect individuals. Security categories are to be used in conjunction with vulnerability and threat information in assessing the risk to organizational operations and assets, individuals, and other organizations. Security categories constitute an initial summary of impact in terms of failures to meet the security objectives of confidentiality, integrity, and availability, and are informed by types of harm.

Task 1-5: Identify Risk Model and Analytic Approach

Identify the risk model and analytic approach to be used in the risk assessment. Organizations need to define one or more risk models for use in conducting risk assessments and identify which model is to be used for the risk assessment. To facilitate reciprocity of assessment results, organization-specific risk models include, or can be translated into, the risk factors (i.e., threat, vulnerability, impact, likelihood, and predisposing condition). Organizations also identify the specific analytic approach to be used for the risk assessment including the assessment approach (i.e., quantitative, qualitative) and the analysis approach (i.e., threat-oriented, asset/impact-oriented, vulnerability-oriented). Organizations typically define the assessment scales to be used in their risk assessments and can identify different assessment scales to be used in different circumstances. For example, for low-impact information systems, organizations could use qualitative values, while for moderate- and high-impact systems, the most granular semiquantitative values (0–100) could be used. As discussed in NIST Special Publication 800-39, Task 1-1, Risk Assumptions, organizations vary in the relative weights applied to risk factors. Therefore, this guideline does not specify algorithms for combining semiquantitative values. Organization-specific risk models include algorithms (e.g., formulas, tables, rules) for combining risk factors. If an organization-specific risk model is not provided in the risk management strategy as part of the risk framing step, then part of this task is to specify the algorithms for combining values. Algorithms for combining risk factors reflect organizational risk tolerance. Organization-specific risk models are refined as part of preparation for a risk assessment by:

- Identifying the risk model and the rationale for using it (when multiple organization-specific risk models are provided);
- Providing additional examples for values of risk factors; and
- Identifying any assessment-specific algorithms.

Key activities – assessment preparation

* Identify the **Purpose** of the risk assessment.
* Identify the **Scope** of the risk assessment.
* Identify the **Assumptions** and **Constraints** under which the risk assessment is conducted.
* Identify **Sources** of threat, vulnerability, and impact information to be used in the risk assessment.
* Define or refine the **Risk Model, Assessment Approach,** and **Analysis Approach** to be used in the risk assessment.

FIGURE 6.6 NIST key activities – assessment preparation.

In the absence of preexisting organization-specific risk models or analytic approaches defined in the organizational risk management strategy, the risk model and analytic approaches to be used in the risk assessment are defined and documented as part of this task (Figure 6.6).

Step 2: Conduct the Assessment

The second step in the risk assessment process is to conduct the assessment with the objective of producing a list of information security risks that can be prioritized by risk level and used to inform risk response decisions. To accomplish this objective, organizations analyze threats and vulnerabilities, impacts and likelihood, and the uncertainty associated with the risk assessment process. This step also involves the gathering of essential information as a part of each task and is conducted in accordance with the assessment context established in the Prepare step of the risk assessment process. The expectation for risk assessments is to adequately cover the entire threat space in accordance with the specific definitions, guidance, and direction established during the Prepare step. However, in practice, adequate coverage within available resources may dictate generalizing threat sources, threat events, and vulnerabilities to ensure full coverage and assessing specific, detailed sources, events, and vulnerabilities only as necessary to accomplish risk assessment objectives. Conducting a risk assessment includes:

* Identifying threat sources relevant to the organization;
* Identifying threat events that could be produced by threat sources;
* Identifying vulnerabilities that could be exploited by threat sources through specific threat events;
* Determining likelihood that threat sources would initiate specific threat events and the likelihood that the threat events would be successful;
* Determining adverse impacts resulting from vulnerability exploitation; and
* Determining information security risks as a combination of likelihood of threat exploitation of vulnerabilities and its associated impact.

Task 2-1: Identify Threat Sources

Identify and characterize threat sources of concern, including capability, intent, and targeting characteristics for adversarial and nonadversarial threats and the range of effects for nonadversarial threats. Organizations need to identify threat sources of concern and determine the characteristics associated with those threat sources. For adversarial threat sources, assess the capabilities, intentions, and targeting associated with the threat sources. For nonadversarial threat sources, assess the potential range of effects from the threat sources. The risk management strategy and the results of the Prepare step provide organizational direction and guidance for conducting threat source identification and characterization including:

- Sources for obtaining threat information;
- Threat sources to consider (by type/name);
- Threat taxonomy to be used; and
- The process for identifying threat sources of concern for the risk assessment.

As identified in Task 1-3, organizations make explicit any assumptions concerning threat sources including decisions regarding the identification of threat sources when specific and credible threat information is unavailable. Organizations can also view adversarial threat sources from a broad-based perspective, considering the time such threat sources may have to exploit identified organizational vulnerabilities, the scale of the attack, and the potential use of multiple attack vectors. The identification and characterization of APTs can involve considerable uncertainty, so organizations should annotate such threat sources with appropriate rationale and references.

Task 2-2: Identify Threat Events

Identify potential threat events, relevance of the events, and the threat sources that could initiate the events. Threat events are characterized by the threat sources that could initiate the events, and, for adversarial events, the procedures used to carry out attacks. Organizations define these threat events with sufficient detail to accomplish the purpose of the risk assessment. At Tier 1, threat events that could affect the organizational level are of particular interest. At Tier 2, threat events that cross or span information system boundaries, exploit functional dependencies or connectivity among systems, or affect mission/business owners are of particular interest. At Tier 3, threat events that can be described in terms of specific information systems, technologies, or operational environments are of particular interest. While multiple threat sources can initiate a single threat event, conversely a single threat source can potentially initiate any of multiple threat events. As a result, there can be a many-to-many relationship among threat events and threat sources that can potentially increase the complexity of the risk assessment. To enable effective use and communication of risk assessment results, organizations tailor the general descriptions of threat events to identify how each event could potentially harm organizational operations (including mission, functions, image, or reputation) and assets, individuals, or other organizations. For each threat event identified, organizations determine the relevance of the event using a range of values. These values have a direct linkage to organizational risk tolerance. The more risk averse, the greater the range of values considered. Organizations accepting greater risk or having a greater risk tolerance are more likely to require substantive evidence before giving serious consideration to threat events. If a threat event is deemed to be irrelevant, no further consideration is given. For relevant threat events, organizations identify all potential threat sources that could initiate the events. For use in Task 2-4, organizations can identify each pairing of threat source and threat event separately since the likelihood of threat initiation and success could be different for each pairing. Alternatively, organizations can identify the set of all possible threat sources that could potentially initiate a threat event.

Task 2-3: Identify Vulnerabilities and Conditions

Identify vulnerabilities and conditions that affect the likelihood that threat events of concern result in adverse impacts. The primary purpose of vulnerability assessments is to understand the nature and degree to which organizations, mission/business processes, and information systems are vulnerable to threat sources identified in Task 2-1 and the threat events identified in Task 2-2 that can be initiated by those threat sources. Vulnerabilities at Tier 1 can be pervasive across organizations and can have wide-ranging adverse impacts if exploited by threat events. For example, organizational failure to consider supply chain activities can result in organizations acquiring subverted components that adversaries could exploit to disrupt organizational missions/business functions or to obtain sensitive organizational information. Vulnerabilities at Tier 2 can be described in terms of organizational mission/business processes, enterprise architecture, the use of multiple information systems, or common infrastructures/shared services. At Tier 2, vulnerabilities typically cross or span information system boundaries. Vulnerabilities at Tier 3 can be described in terms of the information technologies employed within organizational information systems, the environments in which those systems operate, and/or the lack of or weaknesses in system-specific security controls. There is potentially a many-to-many relationship between threat events and vulnerabilities. While multiple threat events can exploit a single vulnerability, conversely multiple vulnerabilities can be exploited by a single threat event. The severity of a vulnerability is based on an assessment of the relative importance of mitigating such a vulnerability. Initially, the extent to which mitigation is unplanned can serve as a surrogate for vulnerability severity. Once the risks associated with a particular vulnerability have been assessed, a gap assessment can be performed to understand the impact severity and exposure of the vulnerability given the security controls implemented and other vulnerabilities can be taken into consideration in assessing vulnerability severity. Assessments of vulnerability severity support risk response. Vulnerabilities can be identified at varying degrees of granularity and specificity. The level of detail provided in any particular vulnerability assessment is consistent with the purpose of the risk assessment and the type of inputs needed to support follow-on likelihood and impact determinations. Due to the ever-increasing size and complexity of organizations, mission/business processes, and the information systems supporting those processes, the number of vulnerabilities tends to be large and can increase the overall complexity of the analysis. Therefore, organizations have the option of using the vulnerability identification task to understand the general nature of the vulnerabilities (including scope, number, and type) relevant to the assessment (see Task 1-3) and performing a cataloging of specific vulnerabilities as necessary to do so. Organizations determine which vulnerabilities are relevant to which threat events in order to reduce the space of potential risks to be assessed. In addition to identifying vulnerabilities, organizations also identify any predisposing conditions that may affect susceptibility to certain vulnerabilities. Predisposing conditions that exist within organizations (including mission/business processes, information systems, and environments of operation) can contribute to (i.e., increase or decrease) the likelihood that one or more threat events, once initiated by threat sources, result in adverse impacts to organizational operations, organizational assets, individuals, or other organizations. Organizations determine which predisposing conditions are relevant to which threat events in order to reduce the space of potential risks to be assessed. Organizations also assess the pervasiveness of predisposing conditions to support determination of the tier(s) at which risk response could be most effective.

Task 2-4: Determine Likelihood

Determine the likelihood that threat events of concern result in adverse impacts, considering:

- The characteristics of the threat sources that could initiate the events;
- The vulnerabilities/predisposing conditions identified; and
- The organizational susceptibility reflecting the safeguards/ countermeasures planned or implemented to impede such events.

Organizations employ a three-step process to determine the overall likelihood of threat events. First, organizations assess the likelihood that threat events will be initiated (for adversarial threat events) or will occur (for nonadversarial threat events). Second, organizations assess the likelihood that threat events once initiated or occurring will result in adverse impacts to organizational operations and assets, individuals, or other organizations. Finally, organizations

Qualitative values	Semi quantitative values		Description
Very high	96–100	10	Adversary is **almost certain** to initiate the threat event
High	80–95	8	Adversary is **highly likely** to initiate the threat event
Moderate	21–79	5	Adversary is **somewhat likely** to initiate the threat event
Low	5–20	2	Adversary is **unlikely** to initiate the threat event
Very low	0–4	0	Adversary is **highly unlikely** to initiate the threat event

FIGURE 6.7 NIST assessment scale – likelihood of threat event initiation (adversarial).

assess the overall likelihood as a combination of likelihood of initiation/occurrence and likelihood of resulting in adverse impact. Organizations assess the likelihood of threat event initiation by taking into consideration the characteristics of the threat sources of concern including capability, intent, and targeting. If threat events require more capability than adversaries possess (and adversaries are cognizant of this fact), then the adversaries are not expected to initiate the events. If adversaries do not expect to achieve intended objectives by executing threat events, then the adversaries are not expected to initiate the events. And finally, if adversaries are not actively targeting specific organizations or their missions/business functions, adversaries are not expected to initiate threat events. Organizations can use the assessment scale in Figure 6.7 and provide a rationale for the assessment allowing explicit consideration of deterrence and threat shifting.

Organizations can also assess the likelihood of threat event occurrence (nonadversarial) using Figure 6.8 and provide a similar rationale for the assessment.

Organizations assess the likelihood that threat events result in adverse impacts by taking into consideration the set of identified vulnerabilities and predisposing conditions (see Task 2-3). For threat events initiated by adversaries, organizations consider characteristics of associated threat sources. For nonadversarial threat events, organizations take into account the anticipated severity and duration of the event. Organizations can use the assessment scale in Figure 6.9 and provide a rationale for the assessment allowing explicit consideration as stated previously.

Threat events for which no vulnerabilities or predisposing conditions are identified have a very low likelihood of resulting in adverse impacts. The overall likelihood of a threat event is a combination of:

- The likelihood that the event will occur (e.g., due to human error or natural disaster) or be initiated by an adversary; and
- The likelihood that the initiation/occurrence will result in adverse impacts.

Qualitative values	Semi quantitative values		Description
Very high	96–100	10	Error, accident, or act of nature is **almost certain** to occur, or **more than 100 times a year**
High	80–95	8	Error, accident, or act of nature is **highly likely** to occur, or occurs **between 10 and 100 times a year**
Moderate	21–79	5	Error, accident, or act of nature is **somewhat likely** to occur, or occurs **between 1 and 10 times a year**
Low	5–20	2	Error, accident, or act of nature is **unlikely** to occur, or occurs **less than once a year, but more than once every 10 years**
Very low	0–4	0	Error, accident, or act of nature is **highly unlikely** to occur, or occurs **less than once every 10 years**

FIGURE 6.8 NIST assessment scale – likelihood of threat event occurrence (nonadversarial).

Task 2-5: Determine Impact

Determine the adverse impacts from threat events of concern considering:

- The characteristics of the threat sources that could initiate the events;
- The vulnerabilities/predisposing conditions identified; and
- The susceptibility reflecting the safeguards/countermeasures planned or implemented to impede such events.

Organizations describe adverse impacts in terms of the potential harm caused to organizational operations and assets, individuals, or other organizations. Where the threat event occurs and whether the effects of the event are contained or spread influence the severity of the impact. Assessing impact can involve identifying assets or potential targets of threat sources, including information resources (e.g., information, data repositories, information systems, applications, information technologies, communications links), people, and physical resources (e.g., buildings, power supplies), which could be affected by threat events. Organizational impacts are defined and prioritized at Tiers 1 and 2, and communicated to Tier 3 as part of risk framing. At Tier 3, impacts are associated with information system capabilities (e.g., processing, display, communications, storage, and retrieval) and resources (e.g., databases, services, components) that could be compromised.

Qualitative values	Semi quantitative values		Description
Very high	96–100	10	If the threat event is initiated or occurs, it is **almost certain** to have adverse inpacts
High	80–95	8	If the threat event is initiated or occurs, it is **highly likely** to have adverse inpacts
Moderate	21–79	5	If the threat event is initiated or occurs, it is **somewhat likely** to have adverse inpacts
Low	5–20	2	If the threat event is initiated or occurs, it is **unlikely** to have adverse inpacts
Very low	0–4	0	If the threat event is initiated or occurs, it is **highly unlikely** to have adverse inpacts

FIGURE 6.9 NIST assessment scale – likelihood of threat event resulting in adverse impacts.

Task 2-6: Determine Risk

Determine the risk to the organization from threat events of concern considering:

- The impact that would result from the events; and
- The likelihood of the events occurring.

Organizations assess the risks from threat events as a combination of likelihood and impact. Figure 6.10 illustrates this relationship.

The level of risk associated with identified threat events represents a determination of the degree to which organizations are threatened by such events. Organizations make explicit the uncertainty in the risk determinations, including, for example, organizational assumptions and subjective judgments/decisions. Organizations can order the list of threat events of concern by the level of risk determined during the risk assessment – with the greatest attention going to high-risk events. Organizations can further prioritize risks at the same level or with similar scores. Each risk corresponds to a specific threat event with a level of impact if that event occurs. In general, the risk level is typically not higher than the impact level, and likelihood can serve to reduce

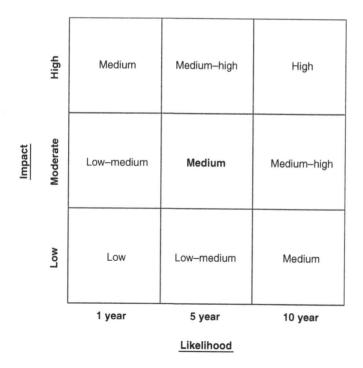

FIGURE 6.10 Likelihood and impact relationship.

risk below that impact level. However, when addressing organization-wide risk management issues with a large number of missions/business functions, mission/business processes, and supporting information systems, impact as an upper bound on risk may not hold. For example, when multiple risks materialize, even if each risk is at the moderate (or medium) level, the set of those moderate-level risks could aggregate to a higher level of risk for organizations. To address situations where harm occurs multiple times, organizations can define a threat event as multiple occurrences of harm and an impact level associated with the cumulative degree of harm. During the execution of Tasks 2-1 to 2-5, organizations capture key information related to uncertainties in risk assessments. These uncertainties arise from sources such as missing information, subjective determinations, and assumptions made. The effectiveness of risk assessment results is in part determined by the ability of decision makers to be able to determine the continued applicability of assumptions made as part of the assessment. Information related to uncertainty is compiled and presented in a manner that readily supports informed risk management decisions. Additionally, guidance should be provided to decision makers for each risk level regarding the estimated time frame (e.g., immediate; 30, 60, 90 days) to select a treatment option (e.g., acceptance, transfer, mitigate, avoid) and implement an appropriate corrective action (or remediation) plan (Figure 6.11).

Step 3: Communicating Risk Assessment Information

The third step in the risk assessment process is to communicate the assessment results and share risk-related information. The objective of this step is to ensure that decision makers across the organization have the appropriate risk-related information needed to inform and guide risk decisions. Communicate risk assessment results to organizational decision makers (e.g., Board, CEO, CIO, CISO/CSO, ISO) to support risk responses. Organizations can communicate risk assessment results in a variety of ways (e.g., executive briefings, risk assessment reports, dashboards, heat maps). Such communications can be formal or informal with the content and format aligning with the organizations' existing risk management reporting process or examples provided within NIST Special Publication 800-30 (Figure 6.12).

Step 4: Maintaining the Assessment

The fourth and final step in the risk assessment process is to maintain the assessment. The objective of this step is to keep current the specific knowledge of the risk organizations incur. The results of risk assessments inform risk management decisions and guide risk responses. To support the ongoing review of risk management decisions (e.g., acquisition decisions, authorization decisions for information systems and common controls, connection decisions), organizations maintain risk assessments to incorporate any changes detected

```
              Key activities – conducting the assessment

  • Identify threat source inputs and threat sources.
  • Determine if threat sources are relevant to the organization and in scope.
  • Create or update the assessment of threat sources.
  • For relevant adversarial threat sources, assess adversary capability, intent, and targeting.
  • For relevant non adversarial threat sources, assess the range of effects from threat sources.
  • Identify vulnerability/predisposing condition inputs and vulnerabilities using organization-
    defined information sources.
  • Assess the severity of identified vulnerabilities.
  • Identify and assess the pervasiveness of predisposing conditions.
  • Identify likelihood determination inputs and factors using organization-defined information
    sources (e.g., threat source characteristics, vulnerabilities, predisposing conditions).
  • Assess the likelihood of threat event initiation for adversarial threats and the likelihood of
    threat event occurrence for non adversarial threats.
  • Assess the likelihood of threat events resulting in adverse impacts, given likelihood of
    initiation or occurrence.
  • Assess the overall likelihood of threat event initiation/occurrence and likelihood of threat
    events resulting in adverse impacts.
  • Identify impact determination inputs and factors using organization-defined information
    sources.
  • Identify adverse impacts and affected assets.
  • Assess the maximum impact associated with the affected assets.
  • Identify risk and uncertainty determination inputs.
  • Determine risk.
```

FIGURE 6.11 NIST key activities – conducting the assessment.

through risk monitoring. Risk monitoring provides organizations with the means to, on an ongoing basis:

- Determine the effectiveness of risk responses;
- Identify risk-impacting changes to organizational information systems and the environments in which those systems operate; and
- Verify compliance.

```
         Key activities – communicating risk assessment information

  • Determine the appropriate method (e.g., executive briefing, risk assessment report, or
    dashboard) to communicate risk assessment results.
  • Communicate risk assessment Results to designated organizational stakeholders.
  • Share the Risk Assessment Results and supporting evidence in accordance with organizational
    policies and guidance.
```

FIGURE 6.12 NIST key activities – communicating risk assessment information.

Maintaining risk assessments includes the following specific tasks:

- Monitor risk factors identified in risk assessments on an ongoing basis and understand subsequent changes to those factors;
- Update the components of risk assessments reflecting the monitoring activities carried out by organizations.

Task 4-1: Monitor Risk Factors

Conduct ongoing monitoring of the risk factors that contribute to changes in risk to organizational operations and assets, individuals, or other organizations. Organizations monitor risk factors of importance on an ongoing basis to ensure that the information needed to make credible, risk-based decisions continues to be available over time. Monitoring risk factors (e.g., threat sources and threat events, vulnerabilities and predisposing conditions, capabilities and intent of adversaries, targeting of organizational operations, assets, or individuals) can provide critical information on changing conditions that could potentially affect the ability of organizations to conduct core missions and business functions. Information derived from the ongoing monitoring of risk factors can be used to refresh risk assessments at whatever frequency deemed appropriate. Organizations can also attempt to capture changes in the effectiveness of risk response measures in order to maintain the currency of risk assessments. The objective is to maintain an ongoing situational awareness of the organizational governance structures and activities, mission/business processes, information systems, and environments of operation, and thereby all of the risk factors that may affect the risk being incurred by organizations. Therefore, in applying the risk assessment context or risk frame (i.e., scope, purpose, assumptions, constraints, risk tolerances, priorities, and trade-offs), organizations consider the part risk factors play in the risk response plan executed. For example, it is expected to be quite common for the security posture of information systems (i.e., the risk factors measured within those systems) to reflect only a part of the organizational risk response, with response actions at the organization level or mission/business process level providing a significant portion of that response. In such situations, monitoring only the security posture of information systems would likely not provide sufficient information to determine the overall risk being incurred by organizations. Highly capable, well-resourced, and purpose-driven threat sources can be expected to defeat commonly available protection mechanisms (e.g., by bypassing or tampering with such mechanisms). Thus, process-level risk response measures such as reengineering mission/business processes, wise use of information technology, or the use of alternate execution processes, in the event of compromised information systems, can be major elements of organizational risk response plans.

Task 4-2: Update Risk Assessment

Update existing risk assessment using the results from ongoing monitoring of risk factors. Organizations determine the frequency and the circumstances

---

Key activities – maintaining the assessment

- Identify key **Risk Factors** that have been identified for ongoing monitoring.
- Identify the **Frequency** of risk factor monitoring activities and the **Circumstances** under which the risk assessment needs to be updated.
- Reconfirm the **Purpose, Scope**, and **Assumptions** of the risk assessment.
- Conduct the appropriate risk assessment **Tasks**, as needed.
- Communicate the subsequent risk assessment **Results** to specified organizational personnel.

FIGURE 6.13 NIST key activities – maintaining the assessment.

under which risk assessments are updated. Such determinations can include, for example, the current level of risk to, and/or the importance of, core organizational missions/business functions. If significant changes (as defined by organizational policies, direction, or guidance) have occurred since the risk assessment was conducted, organizations can revisit the purpose, scope, assumptions, and constraints of the assessment to determine whether all tasks in the risk assessment process need to be repeated. Otherwise, the updates constitute subsequent risk assessments, identifying and assessing only how selected risk factors have changed, for example:

- The identification of new threat events, vulnerabilities, predisposing conditions, undesirable consequences and/or affected assets; and
- The assessments of threat source characteristics (e.g., capability, intent, targeting, range of effects), likelihoods, and impacts.

Organizations communicate the results of subsequent risk assessments to entities across all risk management tiers to ensure that responsible organizational officials have access to critical information needed to make ongoing risk-based decisions (Figure 6.13).

RISK RESPONSE AND REMEDIATION

Risk response identifies, evaluates, decides on, and implements appropriate courses of corrective action to accept, avoid, mitigate, or transfer risk to organizational operations and assets, individuals, and other organizations, resulting from the operation and use of information systems. Identifying and analyzing alternative courses of action typically occurs at Tier 1 or 2. This is due to the fact that alternative courses of action (i.e., potential risk responses) are evaluated in terms of anticipated organization-wide impacts and the ability of organizations to continue to successfully carry out organizational missions and business functions. Decisions to employ risk response measures organization-wide are typically made at Tier 1, although the decisions are informed by risk-related information from the lower tiers. At Tier 2, alternative courses of corrective action are evaluated in terms of anticipated impacts on organizational missions/business functions, the associated mission/business processes supporting the missions/business functions, and resource requirements. At Tier 3, alternative courses of corrective action tend to be evaluated in terms of the system development life cycle or the maximum amount of time available for implementing the selected course(s) of action. The breadth of potential risk responses is a major factor for whether the activity is carried out at Tier 1, 2, or 3. Risk decisions are influenced by organizational risk tolerance developed as part of risk framing activities at Tier 1. Organizations can implement risk decisions at any of the risk management tiers with different objectives and utility of information produced.

Risk Response Identification

Identify alternative courses of action to respond to risk determined during the risk assessment. Organizations can respond to or treat risk in a variety of ways including risk acceptance, avoidance, mitigation, or transfer. A course of action is a time-phased or situation-dependent combination of risk response measures. For example, in an emergency situation, organizations might accept the risk associated with unfiltered connection to an external communications provider for a limited time, and then avoid risk by cutting the connection, mitigate risk in the near term by applying security controls to search for malware or evidence of unauthorized access to information that occurred during the period of unfiltered connection, and finally mitigate risk in the long term by applying controls to handle such connections more securely.

Evaluation of Alternatives

Evaluate alternative courses of action for responding to risk. The evaluation of alternative courses of action can include the expected effectiveness in achieving desired risk response (and how effectiveness is measured and monitored) and anticipated feasibility of implementation, including, for example, mission/business impact, political, legal, social, financial, technical, and economic considerations. Economic considerations include costs throughout the expected period of time during which the course of action is followed (e.g., cost of procurement, integration into organizational processes at Tier 1 and/or 2, information systems at Tier 3, training, and maintenance). During the evaluation of alternative courses of action, trade-offs can be made explicit between near-term gains in mission/business effectiveness or efficiency and long-term risk of mission/business harm due to compromise of information or information systems that are providing this near-term benefit.

Risk Response Decision

Decide on the appropriate course of action for responding to risk. Decisions on the most appropriate course of action include some form of prioritization. Some risks may be of greater concern than other risks. In that case, more resources may need to be directed at addressing higher-priority risks than at other lower-priority risks. This does not necessarily mean that the lower-priority risks would not be addressed. Rather, it could mean that fewer resources might be directed at the lower-priority risks (at least initially), or that the lower-priority risks would be addressed at a later time. A key part of the risk decision process is the recognition that regardless of the decision, there still remains a degree of residual risk that must be addressed. Organizations determine acceptable degrees of residual risk based on organizational risk tolerance and the specific risk tolerances of particular decision makers. Impacting the decision process are some of the more intangible risk-related concepts (e.g., risk tolerance, trust, and culture). The specific beliefs and approaches that organizations embrace with respect to these risk-related concepts affect the course of action selected by decision makers.

Risk Response Implementation

Implement the course of action selected to respond to risk. Once a course of action is selected, organizations implement the associated risk response. Given the size and complexity of some organizations, the actual implementation of risk response measures may be challenging. Some risk response measures are tactical in nature (e.g., applying patches to identified vulnerabilities in organizational information systems) and may be implemented rather quickly. Other risk response measures may be more strategic in nature and reflect solutions that take much longer to implement. Therefore, organizations apply, and tailor as appropriate to a specific risk response course of action, the risk response implementation considerations in the risk response strategies (part of the risk management strategy developed during the risk framing step).

Types of Controls

As reviewed in Chapter 5, there are three categories of controls (or safeguards):

Administrative: Actions, policies, and procedures involved in the selection, development, implementation, and maintenance of security measures. These measures support the protection of information and assist with managing the conduct of the workforce in relation to the protection of information.

Physical: Physical measures to protect the organization's electronic information systems, buildings, and equipment from natural and environmental hazards and unauthorized intrusion.

Technical: Technology and associated policy and procedures for its use to protect and control access to information.

Controls Related to Time

Controls related to time generally fall into three categories:

- Preventative
- Detective
- Corrective

Preventative

Preventative controls are designed to be implemented prior to a threat event and reduce and/or avoid the likelihood and potential impact of a successful threat event. Examples of preventative controls include policies, standards, processes, procedures, encryption, firewalls, and physical barriers.

Detective

Detective controls are designed to detect a threat event while it is occurring and provide assistance during investigations and audits after the event has occurred. Examples of detective controls include security event log monitoring, host and network intrusion detection of threat events, and antivirus identification of malicious code.

Corrective

Corrective controls are designed to mitigate or limit the potential impact of a threat event once it has occurred and recover to normal operations. Examples of corrective controls include automatic removal of malicious code by antivirus software, business continuity and recovery plans, and host and network intrusion prevention of threat events.

KEY TERMS

Term	Definition
Assessment procedure	Consists of a set of assessment objectives, each with an associated set of potential assessment methods and assessment objects
Assessment objective	Includes a set of determination statements related to the security control under assessment
Assessment objects	Identify the specific items being assessed and include specifications, mechanisms, activities, and individuals
Assessment methods	Define the nature of the assessor actions and include examine, interview, and test
Examine method	The process of reviewing, inspecting, observing, studying, or analyzing one or more assessment objects (i.e., specifications, mechanisms, or activities)
Interview method	The process of holding discussions with individuals or groups of individuals within an organization to, once again, facilitate assessor understanding, achieve clarification, or obtain evidence

Term	Definition
Test method	The process of exercising one or more assessment objects (i.e., activities or mechanisms) under specified conditions to compare actual with expected behavior
Preventative controls	Designed to be implemented prior to a threat event and reduce and/or avoid the likelihood and potential impact of a successful threat event
Detective controls	Designed to detect a threat event while it is occurring
Corrective controls	Designed to mitigate or limit the potential impact of a threat event once it has occurred and recover to normal operations

Practice Exam

1. Risk assessments are not:
   a. One-time activities with the hope of providing long-term and definitive information
   b. Performed periodically throughout the information life cycle
   c. Designed to protect the confidentiality, integrity, and availability of information
   d. Designed to guide and inform decision makers in their response to risks
2. NIST's Special Publication 800-30:
   a. Provides guidance for assessing the security controls in federal information systems and organizations and building effective security assessment plans
   b. Provides guidance for conducting risk assessments of healthcare information systems and organizations
   c. Provides guidance for interconnecting information technology systems
   d. Provides guidance for conducting risk assessments of federal information systems and organizations
3. The intent of a risk assessment is to inform decision makers and support risk responses by identifying all of the following except:
   a. Relevant threats to an organization
   b. Internal and external vulnerabilities
   c. Potential impact resulting from a vulnerability exploiting a threat
   d. Likelihood that impact will occur or be realized
4. An assessment procedure consists of:
   a. A set of assessment objectives
   b. An associated set of potential assessment methods
   c. An associated set of assessment objects
   d. All of the above
5. Assessment methods define the nature of the assessor actions and include all of the following methods except:
   a. Interview
   b. Evaluate

     c. Examine

     d. Test

6. The four steps to assessing information security risk include all of the following except:

     a. Prepare for the assessment.

     b. Conduct the assessment.

     c. Remediate assessment findings.

     d. Maintain the assessment.

7. Which of the following is correct?

     a. The Tier 1 context and the system development life cycle determine the purpose and define the scope of risk assessment activities at Tier 2.

     b. At Tier 1, risk assessments support organizational strategies, policies, guidance, and processes for managing risk.

     c. At Tier 3, risk assessments support the determination of mission/business process protection and resiliency requirements, and the allocation of those requirements to the enterprise architecture as part of mission/business segments (that support mission/business processes).

     d. At Tier 3, risk assessments support organizational strategies, policies, guidance, and processes for managing risk.

8. Risk assessments include:

     a. Assessment approaches (i.e., quantitative, qualitative)

     b. Analysis approaches (i.e., threat-oriented, asset/impact-oriented, vulnerability-oriented)

     c. All of the above

     d. None of the above

9. Step 2 of the risk assessment process includes all of the following except:

     a. Identifying threat sources relevant to the organization

     b. Identifying risk model and analytic approach

     c. Identifying vulnerabilities that could be exploited by threat sources through specific threat events

     d. Determining adverse impacts resulting from vulnerability exploitation

10. Step 1 of the risk assessment process includes all of the following except:

     a. Identifying threat sources relevant to the organization

     b. Identifying purpose

     c. Identifying risk model and analytic approach

     d. Identifying scope

11. Risk monitoring provides organizations with the means to, on an ongoing basis:

     a. Identify risk-impacting changes to organizational information systems and the environments in which those systems operate

     b. Verify compliance

     c. Determine the effectiveness of risk responses

     d. All of the above

12. Three types of controls (or safeguards) include all of the following except:
    a. Physical
    b. Tactical
    c. Administrative
    d. Technical

13. Controls related to time generally fall into which of the following categories?
    a. Corrective
    b. Detective
    c. Preventative
    d. All of the above

14. The examine method of assessment is:
    a. The process of exercising one or more assessment objects (i.e., activities or mechanisms) under specified conditions to compare actual with expected behavior
    b. The process of reviewing, inspecting, observing, studying, or analyzing one or more assessment objects (i.e., specifications, mechanisms, or activities)
    c. The process of holding discussions with individuals or groups of individuals within an organization to, once again, facilitate assessor understanding, achieve clarification, or obtain evidence
    d. a and b

15. The interview method of assessment is:
    a. The process of reviewing, inspecting, observing, studying, or analyzing one or more assessment objects (i.e., specifications, mechanisms, or activities)
    b. The process of holding discussions with individuals or groups of individuals within an organization to, once again, facilitate assessor understanding, achieve clarification, or obtain evidence
    c. The process of exercising one or more assessment objects (i.e., activities or mechanisms) under specified conditions to compare actual with expected behavior
    d. None of the above

16. The test method of assessment is:
    a. The process of holding discussions with individuals or groups of individuals within an organization to, once again, facilitate assessor understanding, achieve clarification, or obtain evidence
    b. The process of reviewing, inspecting, observing, studying, or analyzing one or more assessment objects (i.e., specifications, mechanisms, or activities)
    c. The process of exercising one or more assessment objects (i.e., activities or mechanisms) under specified conditions to compare actual with expected behavior
    d. a, b, and c

Practice Exam Answers

1. a
2. d
3. c
4. d
5. b
6. c
7. a
8. c
9. b
10. a
11. d
12. b
13. d
14. d
15. b
16. c

References

National Institute of Standards and Technology, n.d. Guide for Conducting Risk Assessments. NIST Computer Security Publications – NIST Special Publications (SPs). Version SP 800-30 rev1. Web. June 29, 2014. <http://csrc.nist.gov/publications/nistpubs/800-30-rev1/sp800_30_r1.pdf>.

International Organization for Standardization, n.d. Home. ISO/IEC 27005:2011. Web. July 1, 2014. <http://www.iso.org/iso/home/store/catalogue_ics/catalogue_detail_ics.htm?csnumber(56742>.

Health Information Trust Alliance, n.d. Common Security Framework – HITRUST. HITRUST. Web. July 1, 2014. <http://hitrustalliance.net/common-security-framework/>.

National Institute of Standards and Technology, n.d. Managing Information Security Risk. N.p., web. July 1, 2014. <http://csrc.nist.gov/publications/nistpubs/800-39/SP800-39-final.pdf>.

National Institute of Standards and Technology, n.d. An Introductory Resource Guide for Implementing the Health Insurance Portability and Accountability Act (HIPAA) Security Rule. N.p., web. July 1, 2014. <http://csrc.nist.gov/publications/nistpubs/800-66-Rev1/SP-800-66-Revision1.pdf>.

Department of Health and Human Services, n.d. Security Standards: Administrative Safeguards. HIPAA Security Series. Web. July 1, 2014. <http://www.hhs.gov/ocr/privacy/hipaa/administrative/securityrule/adminsafeguards.pdf>.

HIPAA Privacy, Security, and Breach Notification Audit Program, n.d. HIPAA Privacy, Security, and Breach Notification Audit Program. N.p., web. July 31, 2014. <http://www.hhs.gov/ocr/privacy/hipaa/enforcement/audit/>.

National Institute of Standards and Technology, n.d. Guide for Assessing the Security Controls in Federal Information Systems and Organizations. N.p., web. July 1, 2014. <http://csrc.nist.gov/publications/nistpubs/800-53A-rev1/sp800-53A-rev1-final.pdf>.

CHAPTER 7

Third-Party Risk Management

THIS CHAPTER WILL HELP CANDIDATES:

- Understand definition of third parties
- Understand importance of third-party inventory
- Identify and implement third-party standards and practices
- Determine need for third-party assessments
- Coordinate incident response with third parties
- Establish third-party connectivity
- Identify and correct third-party risks

INTRODUCTION

As few healthcare organizations successfully operate without enlisting support from third-party service providers who will access, process, or store patient information, healthcare organizations must understand their responsibilities and proactively manage risks associated with these relationships. To do so, healthcare organizations must understand the definition and maintain an inventory of third parties, apply management standards and practices, identify need for and conduct third-party assessments, implement incident response plans and procedures, establish secure connectivity, and oversee risk management and completion of corrective action plans.

Knowledge Areas

After reviewing this chapter and supporting reference materials, HCISPP candidates should comprehend the importance and purpose of conducting third-party risk assessments. This includes the definition of third parties, identifying assessment requirements, application of management standards and practices, incident response involving third parties, and third-party risk management activities.

167

DEFINITION OF THIRD PARTIES

By law, the HIPAA Privacy Rule applies only to covered (primary) entities including health plans, healthcare clearinghouses, and certain healthcare providers. However, most healthcare providers and health plans do not carry out all of their healthcare activities and functions by themselves. Instead, they often use the services of a variety of other persons or businesses (third parties). The Privacy Rule allows covered entities to disclose protected health information to these third parties (referred to as "business associates") if the covered entities obtain satisfactory assurances that the third party will use the information only for the purposes for which it was engaged by the covered entity, will safeguard the information from misuse, and will help the covered entity comply with some of the covered entity's duties under the Privacy Rule.

For the purpose of this chapter, remember the following definitions:

- **Covered entity**: The primary entity such as a health plan, healthcare clearinghouse, and certain healthcare providers who maintains a direct relationship with patients.
- **Third parties**: Also referred to as business associates, a person or entity that performs certain functions or activities that involve the use or disclosure of protected health information on behalf of, or provides services to, a covered entity. Third parties can also be subcontractors that create, receive, maintain, or transmit protected health information on behalf of another business associate.

INVENTORY

Covered entities are responsible for creating and maintaining an inventory over time of third parties involved in the processing, storage, and/or transmission of their health information. The third-party inventory should also include additional details of importance such as:

- Name of the individual or department who will be responsible for coordinating the execution of business associate or other agreements;
- List of systems and information processed, stored, and/or transmitted by the third party including data classification;
- Details regarding connectivity and/or data exchanges with the third party; and
- Description of services to be provided by the third party such as:
  - Claims processing or billing;
  - Data analysis;
  - Utilization review;
  - Quality assurance;

- Benefit management;
- Practice management;
- Repricing;
- Hardware maintenance; or
- All other HIPAA-regulated functions.

It is important to clearly define roles and responsibilities for the covered entity relationship manager and the third party who will process, store, and/or transmit health information. These roles and responsibilities can be defined within the covered entity's organizational policies and standards and included in contractual agreements (e.g., business associate) where applicable to the third party.

MANAGEMENT STANDARDS AND PRACTICES

When establishing third-party relationships, contractual agreements are required to clearly communicate roles, responsibilities, and requirements pertaining to protecting the confidentiality, integrity, and availability of health information. Under HIPAA, written contracts must be implemented to address:

- **Permitted use**: Establish the permitted and required uses and disclosures of protected health information by the third party
- **Unauthorized disclosure**: Provide that the third party will not use or further disclose the information other than as permitted or required by the contract or as required by law
- **Safeguards**: Require the third party to implement appropriate administrative, physical, and technical safeguards to prevent unauthorized use or disclosure of the information, including implementing requirements of the HIPAA Security Rule with regard to electronic protected health information
- **Event notification**: Require the third party to report to the covered entity any use or disclosure of the information not provided for by its contract, including incidents that constitute breaches of unsecured protected health information
- **Disclosure authorization**: Require the third party to disclose protected health information as specified in its contract to satisfy a covered entity's obligation with respect to individuals' requests for copies of their protected health information, as well as make available protected health information for amendments (and incorporate any amendments, if required) and accountings
- **Compliance**: To the extent the third party is to carry out a covered entity's obligation under the Privacy Rule, require the third party to comply with the requirements applicable to the obligation

- **Audit**: Require the third party to make available to the covered entity and regulatory bodies its internal practices, books, and records relating to the use and disclosure of protected health information received from, or created or received by the third party on behalf of, the covered entity for purposes of determining the covered entity's compliance with the HIPAA Privacy Rule
- **Termination**: At termination of the contract, if feasible, require the third party to return or destroy all protected health information received from, or created or received by the third party on behalf of, the covered entity
- **Subcontractors**: Require the third party to ensure that any subcontractors it may engage on its behalf that will have access to protected health information agree to the same restrictions and conditions that apply to the third party with respect to such information
- **Right to terminate**: Authorize termination of the contract by the covered entity if the third party violates a material term of the contract

It is also important to understand the specific locations/countries where information will be processed, stored, or transmitted. In situations where third-party services involve processing, storage, or transmission of health information outside the covered entity's home country, agreements will need to address jurisdictional matters and additional agreements may be required to ensure compliance with regulatory obligations such as the European Data Protection Directive.

RISK ASSESSMENT

While legal requirements will vary based on local and regional regulations, generally risk assessments are triggered when a third party will process, store, and/or transmit personal health information or by contractual requirements. However, in order to conduct these assessments, a covered entity will need an agreement in place with a third party that addresses:

- Assessment scope (what information is required to complete the assessment, will an on-site inspection of controls be required, etc.);
- Notification requirements (will the third party receive 30/60/90 days' advance notice of an assessment);
- Roles and responsibilities for conducting an assessment (will the assessment be performed by the covered entity or an independent third party);
- Frequency assessments will be performed (annually, biannually, on request, etc.); and

Threat Source Type	Description
ADVERSARIAL Individual: Outsider, Insider, Trusted Insider, Privileged Insider Group: Ad hoc, Established Organization: Competitor, Supplier, Partner, Customer Nation-State	Individuals, groups, organizations, or states that seek to exploit the organization's dependence on cyber resources.
ACCIDENTAL User & Privileged User/Administrator	Erroneous actions taken by individuals in the course of executing their everyday responsibilities.
STRUCTURAL IT Equipment: Storage, Processing, Communications, Display, Sensor Environmental Controls: Temperature/Humidity, Power Supply Software: Operating System, Networking, Application	Failures of equipment, environmental controls, or software due to aging, resource depletion, or other circumstances exceeding expected operating parameters.
ENVIRONMENTAL Natural or Man-Made Disaster: Fire, Flood, Earthquake, Bombing Unusual Natural Event Infrastructure Failure/Outage: Telecommunications, Power	Natural disasters and failures of critical infrastructures on which the organization depends, but which are outside the control of the organization.

FIGURE 7.1 Sample of NIST key activities for HIPAA Security Rule.

- Remediation of findings (how will remediation be handled, will findings trigger a right to terminate agreement for cause if not remediated, etc.).

ASSESSMENT AND AUDIT SUPPORT

While requirements for third-party information asset protection controls will vary by covered entity, scope of services and information, and regulatory requirements, they will generally align with the objectives of the covered entity's information governance and risk management program. Figure 7.1 provides a sample from NIST Special Publication 800-66 Revision 1 of the key administrative, physical, and technical controls and activities required under the HIPAA Security Rule. While all controls may not be required for third parties, it can serve as a guide to assist covered entities with identifying applicable controls, communicating requirements, and monitoring ongoing compliance.

Security Management Process

Key Activities	Description
Identify relevant information systems	- Identify all information systems that house EPHI - Include all hardware and software that are used to collect, store, process, or transmit EPHI - Analyze business functions and verify ownership and control of information system elements as necessary
Conduct risk assessment	- Conduct an accurate and thorough assessment of the potential risks and vulnerabilities to the confidentiality, integrity, and availability of EPHI held by the third party (refer to Chapter 6 for risk assessment methodology)
Implement a risk management program	- Implement security measures sufficient to reduce risks and vulnerabilities to a reasonable and appropriate level

Security Management Process

Key Activities	Description

Acquire IT systems and services	■ Although the HIPAA Security Rule does not require purchasing any particular technology, additional hardware, software, or services may be needed to adequately protect information. Considerations for their selection should include the following:
	  • Applicability of the IT solution to the intended environment
	  • The sensitivity of the data
	  • The organization's security policies, procedures, and standards
	  • Other requirements such as resources available for operation, maintenance, and training

Create and deploy policies and procedures	■ Implement the decisions concerning the management, operational, and technical controls selected to mitigate identified risks ■ Create policies that clearly establish roles and responsibilities and assign ultimate responsibility for the implementation of each control to particular individuals or offices ■ Create procedures to be followed to accomplish particular security-related tasks
Develop and implement a sanction policy	■ Apply appropriate sanctions against workforce members who fail to comply with the security policies and procedures of the third party ■ Develop policies and procedures for imposing appropriate sanctions (e.g., reprimand, termination) for noncompliance with the organization's security policies ■ Implement sanction policy as cases arise
Develop and deploy the information system activity review process	■ Implement procedures to regularly review records of information system activity such as audit logs, access reports, and security incident tracking reports
Develop appropriate standard operating procedures	■ Determine the types of audit trail data and monitoring procedures that will be needed to derive exception reports
Implement the information system activity review and audit process	■ Activate the necessary review process ■ Begin auditing and logging activity

Assigned Security Responsibilities

Key Activities	Description
Select a security official to be assigned responsibility for HIPAA security	■ Identify the individual who has final responsibility for security ■ Select an individual who is able to assess effective security and to serve as the point of contact for security policy, implementation, and monitoring

Assigned Security Responsibilities

Key Activities	Description
Assign and document the individual's responsibility	■ Document the assignment to one individual's responsibilities in a job description ■ Communicate this assigned role to the entire organization

Workforce Security

Key Activities	Description
Implement procedures for authorization and/or supervision	■ Implement procedures for the authorization and/or supervision of workforce members who work with EPHI or in locations where it might be accessed
Establish clear job descriptions and responsibilities	■ Define roles and responsibilities for all job functions ■ Assign appropriate levels of security oversight, training, and access ■ Identify in writing who has the business need – and who has been granted permission – to view, alter, retrieve, and store EPHI, and at what times, under what circumstances, and for what purposes
Establish criteria and procedures for hiring and assigning tasks	■ Ensure that staff members have the necessary knowledge, skills, and abilities to fulfill particular roles ■ Ensure that these requirements are included as part of the personnel hiring process
Establish a workforce clearance procedure	■ Implement procedures to determine that the access of a workforce member to EPHI is appropriate ■ Implement appropriate screening of persons who will have access to EPHI ■ Implement a procedure for obtaining clearance from appropriate offices or individuals where access is provided or terminated
Establish termination procedures	■ Implement procedures for terminating access to EPHI when the employment of a workforce member ends or as required ■ Develop a standard set of procedures that should be followed to recover access control devices (e.g., identification badges, access cards) ■ Deactivate computer access accounts

Information Access Management

Key Activities	Description
Isolate healthcare clearinghouse functions	■ If a healthcare clearinghouse is part of a larger organization, the clearinghouse must implement policies and procedures that protect the EPHI of the clearinghouse from unauthorized access by the larger organization ■ Determine if a component of the third party constitutes a healthcare clearinghouse under the HIPAA Security Rule ■ If no clearinghouse functions exist, document this finding. If it does, ensure implementation of procedures for access consistent with the HIPAA Privacy Rule

Information Access Management

Key Activities	Description
Implement policies and procedures for authorizing access	■ Implement policies and procedures for granting access to EPHI, for example, through access to a workstation, transaction, program, process, or other mechanism ■ Decide how access will be granted to workforce members within the organization ■ Select the basis for restricting access ■ Select an access control method (e.g., identity-based, role-based) ■ Determine if direct access to EPHI will ever be appropriate for individuals external to the organization (e.g., third parties, subcontractors)
Implement policies and procedures for access establishment and modification	■ Implement policies and procedures that, based on the organization's access authorization policies, establish, document, review, and modify a user's right of access to a workstation, transaction, program, or process ■ Establish standards for granting access ■ Provide formal authorization from the appropriate authority before granting access to sensitive information
Evaluate existing security measures related to access controls	■ Evaluate the security features of access controls already in place, or those of any planned for implementation, as appropriate ■ Determine if these security features involve alignment with other existing management, operational, and technical controls, such as policy standards and personnel procedures, maintenance and review of audit trails, identification and authorization of users, and physical access controls

Communication of Findings

Findings resulting from completed third-party assessments should be clearly communicated to management at both the covered entity and third party. Treatment decisions and action plans should be agreed between the parties, documented in writing, and formally tracked until remediation has been completed.

INCIDENT NOTIFICATION AND RESPONSE

Attacks frequently compromise personal and business data, and it is critical to respond quickly and effectively when security incidents occur. The concept of incident response has become widely accepted and implemented. One of the benefits of having an incident response capability is that it supports responding to incidents systematically (i.e., following a consistent incident handling methodology) so that appropriate actions are taken. Incident response helps organizations to minimize loss or theft of information and disruption of services, and reduce overall risk associated with incidents. Another benefit is the ability to use information gained during incident handling to help the organization better prepare for handling future incidents and provide stronger protection for systems and data. Sound incident response capabilities also help in dealing with legal issues that may arise during or after incidents.

Internal Processes for Incident Response

Organizations should define and implement policies, processes, and procedures to appropriately address security incidents in a timely manner as they arise. As described in NIST's Special Publication 800-61 Revision 2, Computer Security Incident Handling Guide, the incident response process includes several phases. The initial phase involves establishing and training an incident response team, and acquiring the necessary tools and resources. During preparation, the organization also attempts to limit the number of incidents that will occur by selecting and implementing a set of controls based on the results of risk assessments. However, residual risk will inevitably persist after controls are implemented. Detection of security breaches is thus necessary to alert the organization whenever incidents occur. In keeping with the severity of the incident, the organization can mitigate the impact of the incident by containing it and ultimately recovering from it. During this phase, activity often cycles back to detection and analysis, for example, to see if additional hosts are infected by malware while eradicating a malware incident. After the incident is adequately handled, the organization issues a report that details the cause and cost of the incident and the steps the organization should take to prevent future incidents. Figure 7.2 illustrates the relationship between the various phases during the incident response life cycle.

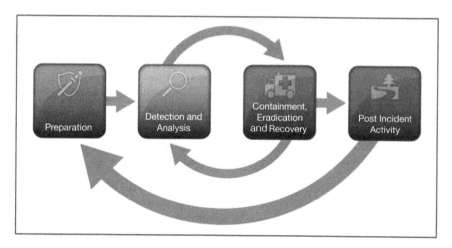

FIGURE 7.2 NIST incident response life cycle.

Incident Response Relationship Between Covered Entity and Third Party

Strong relationships, contractually defined roles and responsibilities, and close coordination are critical between covered entities and third parties when incidents occur. Roles and responsibilities should be clearly defined and requirements included within contractual agreements where appropriate such as:

- Notification point(s) of contact;
- Expectations regarding timely notification of incidents; and
- Agreements to cooperate and mitigate potential covered entity risk.

Third parties must provide a reasonable assurance of being able to report suspected incidents to a covered entity in a timely manner so a covered entity can initiate its own incident response process and procedures.

Breach Identification, Notification, and Initial Response

Depending on where a covered entity conducts business, it may have to comply with various local, state, and/or federal regulations that require notification of suspected incidents within a specific time frame. As a regulatory notification clock can start from the time an incident was identified, it is increasingly important that third parties notify a covered entity of an incident as soon as reasonably possible. For example, the HIPAA Breach Notification Rule requires covered entities and their business associates to provide notification following a breach of unsecured protected health information. Under the rule, notification is required to the affected individuals, the Secretary, and, in certain circumstances, the media. Notification also must occur without unreasonable delay and within 60 days for individuals and 60 days for the Secretary when more than 500 individuals were impacted following the discovery of a breach.

As a result, third-party agreements should clearly communicate breach notification and incident response expectations including point(s) of contact at the primary entity and what information must be reasonably provided to assist with risk assessment and appropriate response activities such as type of information and number of records involved in the breach. Agreements should also address whether the primary entity or third party will be responsible for issuing notifications and that both organizations agree to fully cooperate with and participate in an investigation should either be required.

For situations where an incident has occurred as a result of suspected illegal or malicious activities, law enforcement should be engaged and maintaining evidence chain of custody becomes increasingly important. To maintain chain of custody, you must document the preservation of evidence from the time it is collected to the time it is presented in court. To prove the chain of custody, and ultimately show that the evidence has remained intact, prosecutors will generally need individuals who can testify:

- That the evidence offered in court is the same evidence they collected or received;
- To the time and date the evidence was received or transferred to another provider; and
- That there was no tampering with the item while it was in custody.

ESTABLISHING CONNECTIVITY

Covered entities should ensure completion of risk assessments, treatment of risk, and execution of contractual agreements prior to establishing third-party connectivity. They should also assess their level of trust for the third party and understand requirements for connectivity, system access, and data exchanges to ensure the implementation of appropriate safeguards (or standards) to guard against unauthorized data access.

Trust

A covered entity's level of trust can be assessed based on the results of the covered entity's risk assessment, identified deficiencies, and status of remediation plans. Organizations can also take into consideration information such as a third party's historical track record of protecting information and any assurances provided by an independent and mutually trusted third party. Next, the covered entity needs to understand what (if any) information will be exchanged and the classification (or sensitivity) of the information, always taking care to minimize what is shared to only that which is required. Finally, the organization needs to understand if the third party will require direct access to its systems. If access is required, the third party should be required to comply with the covered entity's policies and access should be granted on a role-based, need-to-know, and least privileged basis.

Safeguards

When establishing third-party connectivity, requirements for administrative, physical, and technical safeguards should be identified. Once identified, controls should be appropriately implemented to protect the confidentiality, integrity, and availability of the covered entity's information and information systems. Refer to Figure 7.1 or NIST Special Publication 800-66 for examples of activities and controls required under the HIPAA Security Rule.

Connection Agreements

Connection agreements can be used to define and mutually agree on the type of connectivity that will be established between the parties. The agreements can also address administrative, physical, and technical safeguards that either party must implement and maintain as a condition of establishing connectivity. These can be either included within a business associate agreement or handled separately.

PROMOTING AWARENESS OF REQUIREMENTS

Information Flow Mapping and Scope

Healthcare organizations need to understand how information flows between systems and within the organization as part of the information life cycle and to support their mission. They also need to understand the role of third parties and how the information they access, process, and store fits into the equation. This will help improve an organization's ability to manage risk and ensure sensitive information is appropriately protected throughout its life cycle, regardless of where it is accessed, processed, or stored.

Data Sensitivity and Classification

To determine the value and risk associated with data, an organization must first assess the confidentiality, integrity, and availability requirements that pertain to the data. These requirements can come from the business, be driven by local, state, and federal regulatory requirements that apply to certain types of data (e.g., electronic personal health information, personally identifiable information), or a combination of both. Not all data types will share the same sensitivity or classification. For example, a patient's name in combination with home address does not share a similar value and present the same risk as a patient's name in combination with Social Security number (SSN). As a result, name in combination with home address might be assigned a *medium* risk classification and require less security controls than name in combination with SSN that might be assigned a *high* risk classification. Different volumes of information can also have an impact on classification. For example, 1 patient's name in combination with SSN would have a different value and risk than the name and SSN of 500 patients.

Once an organization identifies the confidentiality, integrity, and availability of information shared with a third party, it will be better positioned to implement the required safeguards for such information based on its classification.

Privacy Requirements

The HIPAA Privacy Rule establishes national standards to protect individuals' medical records and other personal health information and applies to health plans, healthcare clearinghouses, and those healthcare providers that conduct certain healthcare transactions electronically. The Rule requires appropriate safeguards to protect the privacy of personal health information, and sets limits and conditions on the uses and disclosures that may be made of such information without patient authorization. The Rule also gives patients rights over their health information, including rights to examine and obtain a copy of their health records, and to request corrections. Organizations must assess privacy requirements that apply prior to sharing data with a third party to ensure compliance with business and regulatory requirements.

Security Requirements

The HIPAA Security Rule establishes national standards to protect individuals' electronic personal health information that is created, received, used, or maintained by a covered entity. The Security Rule requires appropriate administrative, physical, and technical safeguards to ensure the confidentiality, integrity, and security of electronic protected health information. Security requirements are closely associated with privacy and can typically be derived based on the classification of data. Once an organization is assigned an appropriate classification based on the confidentiality, integrity, and availability of the data, appropriate administrative, physical, and technical safeguards can be identified to ensure the data are protected.

Risks Associated With Third Parties

The primary healthcare organization is ultimately responsible for the protection of data entrusted to them, whether accessed, processed, or stored internally or shared with their third parties. As such, they must conduct periodic due diligence on their third parties to ensure appropriate administrative, physical, and technical safeguards are implemented to maintain compliance with the primary healthcare organization's requirements.

RISK REMEDIATION

Management, treatment, and corrective action plans associated with third-party risks should be handled and tracked in a manner consistent with the primary healthcare organization's security and privacy governance practices discussed in Chapters 5 and 6. Likelihood and impact of third-party findings should be assessed, corrective action plans developed and communicated, and remediation tracked as part of ongoing compliance activities by the covered entity. Third-party contractual agreements should also clearly address remediation requirements including who will be responsible for any costs associated with remediation. Once a third party provides an attestation of remediation being completed, the primary healthcare organization should review evidence to validate and ensure risks have been remediated to an acceptable level.

KEY TERMS

Term	Definition
Chain of custody	Documenting the preservation of evidence from the time it is collected to the time it is presented in court
Covered entity	The primary entity such as a health plan, healthcare clearinghouse, and certain healthcare providers who maintains a direct relationship with patients
Third party	Also referred to as business associates, a person or entity that performs certain functions or activities that involve the use or disclosure of protected health information on behalf of, or provides services to, a covered entity. Third parties can also be subcontractors that create, receive, maintain, or transmit protected health information on behalf of another business associate
Incident response	Process to help organizations minimize loss or theft of information, disruption of services, and reduce overall risk associated with incidents
Level of trust	Assessed based on the results of the covered entity's risk assessment, identified deficiencies, and status of remediation plans
Connection agreement	Used to define and mutually agree on the type of connectivity that will be established between the parties
HIPAA Privacy Rule	Requires appropriate safeguards to protect the privacy of personal health information, and sets limits and conditions on the uses and disclosures that may be made of such information without patient authorization
HIPAA Security Rule	Establishes national standards to protect individuals' electronic personal health information that is created, received, used, or maintained by a covered entity

Practice Exam

1. The HIPAA Privacy Rule applies only to covered (primary) entities including:
   a. Health plans
   b. Healthcare clearinghouses
   c. Certain healthcare providers
   d. All of the above
2. Under HIPAA, written contracts must be implemented to address:
   a. Termination
   b. Breach reimbursement
   c. Event notification
   d. a and c
3. Risk assessments are generally triggered when a third party will:
   a. Store, process, and/or transmit personal health information
   b. Store and/or process personal health information

    c. Transmit and/or process personal health information

    d. Transmit and/or store personal health information

4. Which NIST Special Publication describes the key administrative, physical, and technical controls and activities required under the HIPAA Security Rule?

    a. 800-61 Revision 2

    b. 800-39

    c. 800-66 Revision 1

    d. 800-30 Revision 1

5. Findings resulting from completed third-party assessments should be clearly communicated to:

    a. Management at the covered entity

    b. Management at the third party

    c. a and b

    d. None of the above

6. Incident response helps organizations to:

    a. Reduce overall risk associated with incidents

    b. Minimize disruption of services

    c. Minimize loss or theft of information

    d. All of the above

7. Which NIST Special Publication focuses on computer security incident response handling?

    a. 800-61 Revision 2

    b. 800-39

    c. 800-66 Revision 1

    d. 800-30 Revision 1

8. Under the HIPAA Breach Notification Rule, notification is generally required to the affected individuals, the Secretary, and in certain circumstances, the media within:

    a. 30 days

    b. 45 days

    c. 60 days

    d. 90 days

9. A covered entity's level of trust for a third party can be assessed based on the results of:

    a. Identified deficiencies

    b. The covered entity's risk assessment

    c. Status of remediation plans

    d. All of the above

10. Connection agreements with third parties can be used to:

    a. Address administrative, physical, and technical safeguard requirements

    b. Define and mutually agree on the type of connectivity established between parties

    c. a and b

    d. None of the above

11. To determine the value and risk associated with data, an organization must assess data:
    a. Confidentiality requirements
    b. Integrity requirements
    c. Availability requirements
    d. All of the above

12. The HIPAA Privacy Rule establishes:
    a. National standards to protect individuals' medical records and other personal health information and applies to health plans, healthcare clearinghouses, and those healthcare providers that conduct certain healthcare transactions electronically
    b. National standards to protect individuals' electronic personal health information that is created, received, used, or maintained by a covered entity
    c. International standards to protect individuals' medical records and other personal health information and applies to health plans, healthcare clearinghouses, and those healthcare providers that conduct certain healthcare transactions electronically
    d. International standards to protect individuals' electronic personal health information that is created, received, used, or maintained by a covered entity

13. The HIPAA Security Rule establishes:
    a. National standards to protect individuals' medical records and other personal health information and applies to health plans, healthcare clearinghouses, and those healthcare providers that conduct certain healthcare transactions electronically
    b. National standards to protect individuals' electronic personal health information that is created, received, used, or maintained by a covered entity
    c. International standards to protect individuals' medical records and other personal health information and applies to health plans, healthcare clearinghouses, and those healthcare providers that conduct certain healthcare transactions electronically
    d. International standards to protect individuals' electronic personal health information that is created, received, used, or maintained by a covered entity

14. Who is ultimately responsible for the protection of data entrusted to a healthcare organization?
    a. Patient
    b. Third party accessing, processing, or storing healthcare data
    c. Primary healthcare organization
    d. Department of Health and Human Services (HHS)

Practice Exam Answers

1. d
2. d
3. a
4. c
5. c
6. d
7. a
8. c
9. d
10. c
11. d
12. a
13. b
14. c

References

Breach Notification Rule, n.d. Breach Notification Rule. N.p., web. September 1, 2014. <http://www.hhs.gov/ocr/privacy/hipaa/administrative/breachnotificationrule/>.

Business Associates. Health Information Privacy. Department of Health & Human Services, December 3, 2002. Web. August 15, 2014. <http://www.hhs.gov/ocr/privacy/hipaa/understanding/coveredentities/businessassociates.pdf>.

Business Associate Contracts, n.d. Business Associate Contracts. N.p., web. September 1, 2014. <http://www.hhs.gov/ocr/privacy/hipaa/understanding/coveredentities/contractprov.html>.

National Institute of Standards and Technology, n.d. An Introductory Resource Guide for Implementing the Health Insurance Portability and Accountability Act (HIPAA) Security Rule. IST Special Publication 800-66 Revision 1. Web. September 1, 2014. <http://csrc.nist.gov/publications/nistpubs/800-66-Rev1/SP-800-66-Revision1.pdf>.

National Institute of Standards and Technology, n.d. Computer Security Incident Handling Guide. Special Publication 800-61 Revision 2. Web. September 1, 2014. <http://csrc.nist.gov/publications/nistpubs/800-61rev2/SP800-61rev2.pdf>.

National Institute of Standards and Technology, n.d. Managing Information Security Risk. N.p., web. July 1, 2014. <http://csrc.nist.gov/publications/nistpubs/800-39/SP800-39-final.pdf>.

SART Toolkit – Develop a SART, n.d. SART Toolkit – Develop a SART. N.p., web. September 1, 2014. <http://ovc.ncjrs.gov/sartkit/develop/issues-coc.html>.

The Security Rule, n.d. The Security Rule. N.p., web. September 1, 2014. <http://www.hhs.gov/ocr/privacy/hipaa/administrative/securityrule/index.html>.

Index

Printed in the United States
By Bookmasters